SoundBites:
A Business Guide for Working with the Media

by Kathy Kerchner

savage

PRESS

Box 115, Superior, WI 54880 (715) 394-9513

First Edition
Printed in 1997

© Copyright 1997
Kathy Kerchner

Cover Design © 1997
Doris Trojan

ISBN 1-886028-30-3

Library of Congress Catalog Card Number: 97-069182

Printed in the U.S.A.
at
Morris Publishing
Kearney, NE

Table of Contents

Introduction   9

1. The All-Important Soundbite 13

The Five C's of Success
What Gets Soundbited
Negligible Nibbles vs.
         Successful Soundbites
What *Not* to Do

2. Building Media Relationships 38

Why Deal with the Media?
Anatomy of a Reporter
Know the Newsroom
Never Say "No Comment"
When to Refuse an Interview
To Be "Off the Record" or Not to Be
Correcting Errors
Ten Essentials of Media Relationships
NewsSpeak Quiz

3. Attracting Reporters to Your Story   88

What is News?
News Hangs on "Hooks"
News Categories
Develop a Media List
Deadline Guidelines
News Releases: Avoid the Circular File
News Release Format
Media Advisory
Fact Sheet

Table of Contents

Press Kit or Media Kit Ingredients
Using Photos for Positive Impact
Media Relations in Cyberspace
Follow-Up
Personal Meetings
Video News Release
Satellite Media Tour
Public Service Announcement
Other Media Needs

4. Preparing for Your Media Interview 142

Buy Time
Know the Territory
Determine What They'll Ask You
Identify Your Agenda
Preparation Checklist

5. Use Proven Answering Techniques 163

The Basics
    Bridge to Your Message
    Stay Positive
    Hold Your Ground
    Show Empathy and Concern
    Invert the Triangle
    Be Concise
    Keep Your Cool
    Avoid Jargon
    Pause

Tricks of the Trade
    Admit Mistakes
    Hesitate to Speculate

Table of Contents

Flag What's Important
Correct False "Facts"
Don't Let Reporters Put Words in
    Your Mouth
Don't Be a Know-It-All
Don't Fill Silences
If You Can't Say Something Nice
Use the Reporter's Name
"Anything You Want to Add?"

6. Watch Your Nonverbal
    Communication   189

Understanding the "3 V's"
Visual Communication
Vocal Communication
The Telephone Interview
Microphone Manners

7. Media Interviews:
    Up Close and Sparkling   212

News Conferences

Television Interviews
    Taped TV News Story
    Live TV News Story
    Live On Set
    TV Interview Show
    Anchor Interview
Print Interviews
    Newspaper Story/Magazine Story

Table of Contents

Editorial Board Meeting

Radio Interviews

Radio Talk Show

Taped Radio Interview/
Live Radio Interview

Interviews in Cyberspace

Post-Interview Evaluation

8. Confronting Crises   230

From Bad to Worse
The Good Get Better Faster
Planning for Crisis
Communicating in Crisis
Managing a Cybercrisis

9. Glory in the SoundBite   263

About the Author   267

Index   268

**Workshops and
        Ordering Information**

Dedication

To Paul Bennett —
teacher, mentor, friend

Acknowledgments

When I was an English major at Denison University in Granville, Ohio, writing professor Paul Bennett borrowed one of the favorite slogans of the 60's ("Right on!") to inspire his students to continuously work at their craft ("Write on!"). When I finally decided to "write on" about *SoundBites*, his collaboration proved invaluable. I couldn't have finished the manuscript without his advice and encouragement (nagging?), nor would the book have been as cogent or complete without his additions to style and content.

My friend Heidi Ream never fails to come up with the right ideas. Knowing that I'd wanted to write this book and that I tend to procrastinate on big projects, she insisted *now* is the time. Thanks to her for reading and responding to many versions, and thanks to my wonderful staff at the Phoenix Speakers Bureau for their never-ending support.

Shirley Brice and Dave Polyard became friends of mine when they worked at a competing TV station (she as a reporter, he as a photographer). Now they're married and living in a different city, but still working in related fields. Their experience and perspective helped me fine-tune the manuscript.

Thanks to Mike Savage who believed this book should be published — and put his money where his mouth is. I also thank Michael LeBouef, Wally Amos, Larry Barton and Linda Blessing for their endorsements.

With a background in both media and public relations, Debra Gelbart has contributed her expertise to my business and my book. I appreciate her insight and friendship.

Thanks to Barbara Wood for her emphasis on research and detail.

Doris Trojan always finds a creative and stylish way to make me look good. Thanks to her for the cover design.

I appreciate the many colleagues who helped me learn the news business over the years — including Steve Corona, Ian Pearson, Reid Chapman, Al Buch, Jim Willi, Dennis Morgino and the Radio/TV/Film professors in my University of Michigan graduate school program.

I am especially indebted to the many friends and clients who helped me make the transition to my career as trainer, speaker and consultant, and who have lived many of the examples in this book...

And to my guardian angel, Ray Fife, who will forever be part of all I accomplish.

Introduction

"Public sentiment is everything. With public sentiment nothing can fail; without it, nothing can succeed." Do you know who said that? It was Abraham Lincoln in the mid-19th century. Today, almost 150 (dare I say "seven score and ten?") years later, those words endure, coloring almost every exchange that makes news. In this century, the news media shape and mold the body of public sentiment. Editors and reporters decide what to feed us in our daily information diet. They influence our opinions and perspectives, sway our emotions, and impact our destinies.

During my 14 years as a TV news reporter and anchor, I often wondered why the people I interviewed didn't do a better job. The better they did, the better my story would be. Why, I asked myself, didn't they take advantage of the opportunity I was giving them to communicate their messages? Why didn't they learn more about what works with the media and what doesn't? When I left broadcasting, I decided to form a company (Kathy Kerchner InterSpeak, Inc.) that would help people make the most of their media opportunities. This book, based on my 14 years in the media plus nine years of consulting with major corporations, businesses and government, is written to help people do just that.

If you are like the interviewees and clients I have worked with through the years, you probably have trepidations about talking to the news media. You may not trust reporters or the news process itself. You may not know how reporters work or what they think is important. Perhaps, like many people I've interviewed and worked with, you'd rather just ignore the media, hoping they will go away. That's unlikely to happen.

Whether we like it or not, the news media are an integral part of our society protected by our first amendment right to free speech. News is everywhere. You can hardly avoid it. Television and radio stations are expanding news broadcasts. Newspapers have intensified their coverage of business and industry. Chances are, whatever career you follow, at some time you are going to want or have to deal with the news media. To be effective in what may be your 15 minutes of fame or even fame that is a daily ritual, you'll need to speak clearly, concisely and colorfully. This book presents scores of tips and strategies for making the most of every media moment.

Perhaps some of you, thinking as I once thought, assume we can change the media or alter how reporters do their jobs. Not likely. Indeed, we probably could spend days talking about how the media *should* be different. Often I hear complaints from my clients: *Why don't reporters do their homework? Why do they focus on negative topics? How can they expect to tell a story in such a short time or in so few words?* These are all valid criticisms. I, like most reporters, sometimes experienced frustration with the limitations and restraints of the news business.

While complaining may make us feel bet-

Introduction

ter, ultimately it won't help. Neither you nor I can change the media. But we do have the power to change ourselves and how we deal with reporters. Since the media can have such a significant impact on our business or personal lives, we'd better learn how they think, act and react. The way you respond to an interview request, the way you conduct yourself during the interview, what you feel, think and say does much to determine how the reporter responds and how the story turns out. As the media/business relationship evolves, one must adapt to survive.

You really can develop skills to make your media experience successful. That's what this book is about. I'll show you how to play the media's game to *your* advantage. But this book is not a magic potion. Reading it and accepting its major tenets will not automatically make you a master of the media. There is no substitute for hands-on experience and personal coaching. If, however, you actually put into practice the things I talk about, if you work consistently on media techniques, you will significantly increase your likelihood of success.

SoundBites: A Business Guide for Working with the Media will make demands of you. Time and effort spent on it will yield a growing competency in communicating with the public. You and your business or organization may be doing an excellent, responsible job in the community, but what you are doing doesn't count until public perception confirms it. Lincoln said, "Public sentiment is everything." At the risk of putting words into the mouth of a great president who was also a media expert, today Lincoln might say, "Public sentiment, rendered by the media, is everything."

With the secrets that you'll discover in *SoundBites*, you can deal effectively with the media. You can manage public sentiment to help mold perception into reality. And, when your key moments arrive, you'll be ready to deliver clear, strong soundbites with real staying power.

Chapter 1

The All-Important Soundbite

As long as we've been speaking and writing, we humans have been intrigued by the pithy saying, the unusual turn of phrase and the interesting insight. Those who comprehend the great sweep of civilization and history would tell us that the soundbite is an electronic version of the way communication has always occurred. They will cite philosophers, shamans, poets, holy men — the great body of word smiths — as the first to use soundbites. To be more specific, they might cite the poet Sappho, writing her aphoristic poetry in Greece in 6th century B.C.:

> I cannot, dearest mother, my loom I cannot mind;
> Delicate Aphrodite with longing leaves me blind.
>
> The fairest apple glistens, high against the sky,
> High on the topmost branch, where the pickers
> passed it by.
> Forgotten? Oh, no, not forgotten.
> They never could reach so high.

They might cite this enduring truth from the great body of wisdom of the Grecian philosopher Socrates in 5th century BC:

> "Children today are tyrants. They contradict their

SoundBites

parents, gobble their food, and tyrannize their teachers."

They might turn to Socrates' famous pupil and biographer, Plato:

"Those who are too smart to engage in politics are punished by being governed by those who are dumber."

The world today reckons with a similar need to transmit insightful, basic human truths, but to far greater numbers of people than were reached by the great oral communicators of the past. Our modern world instantly conveys these truths to the masses by newspapers, radio, television, and most recently by online computer services. Those who manage these means of communication understand their public. They know Americans are busy and so bombarded with information that it takes exceptional performance to grab our attention. With the proliferation of electronic media, a strange critter called the "soundbite" now dominates our public discourse.

The term *soundbite*, which started as television news jargon, merits being understood by the general public. Here's what it means. A TV reporter interviews you for 15 minutes on something crucial to you or your business. That night on the news, you eagerly await the story and see yourself appear for only six or eight seconds. That small part which the reporter selects from your longer interview is your soundbite.

Chapter One

In the TV media, professionals call the interviewee a "talking head." They loathe talking heads that are boring or might cause viewers to grab the remote control. So, they avoid the long interview in favor of a short, fast-paced story. This story must be visually interesting, one that can be told and shown in a soundbite or two.

USA Today brilliantly capitalized on this trend toward brevity by taking the concept of soundbites to printed form. When the newspaper premiered in September, 1982, critics called it "McPaper," fast-food for the mind. But busy Americans liked the short, bite-sized stories that were complete on one page. The paper revolutionized print journalism with lots of quickly consumable news nuggets, photos, graphics, and sports scores. Editors used splashes of color to punch up the visuals. Other newspapers took up the "make it visual, shorter-is-better" philosophy.

Which, you may ask, came first, the chicken or the egg? Did our attention spans decrease, forcing the media to give us shorter and shorter segments, or did the media give us so many quick bites we developed an appetite for smaller morsels? Probably both. But let's look at what has happened.

Media, competing for our attention, feature shorter than ever soundbites. In 1960, their average length was 40 seconds. Now the average length is 7.2 seconds. One soundbite of that length is often used to summarize an entire interview, event or story. And it works.

In October, 1988, when Lloyd Bentsen and

SoundBites

Dan Quayle were vice presidential candidates, they debated each other before a national TV audience. After Quayle tried to compare himself to former President John F. Kennedy, Bentsen replied with a soundbite which prevailed: "Senator, I knew Jack Kennedy. Jack Kennedy was a friend of mine. And Senator, you're no Jack Kennedy."

In 1995, Attorney Johnnie Cochran's lengthy closing argument for the defense in the O.J. Simpson trial took on soundbite potency in these seven words: "If it doesn't fit, you must acquit."

This quest for soundbites can be frustrating. Those who need to communicate through the media rightfully ask, "How can we hope to make the case for ourselves or our businesses when our statements are dissected into six or eight second parcels of information?"

The first step to success in this vital undertaking is accepting the reality of TV newscasting. It may not be "fair" and it may not be "right" that an interview gets edited down to a soundbite, but that is the way reporters package their stories. They weave your soundbites and soundbites from other sources with their own voice-over narration and on-camera stand-up, which often paraphrase what you said, to create a finished report. That report may run only a minute or so. The typical half-hour news program has in it only eight to ten minutes of actual news. As you would know if you'd have used your stopwatch on your local station's newscast, the bulk of time goes to commercials, teases, sports, weather, program open and program close.

Once you understand the importance of a soundbite and its brevity, you can conduct yourself during an interview to make the most of it. How? By simply planting soundbite nuggets throughout your interview. Most reporters find it difficult to define a soundbite, but any good reporter knows when he or she hears a usable gem. Reporters have a sixth sense about this. In my experience, after an interview was over, while the photographer and I packed up our gear, he would ask me, "Did you get anything?" On a good day, I'd say something like, "I got a couple of bites." On a day when the interviewee showed no awareness of media reporting, I would answer, "Boy, did he (she) blow that chance. Now I have to make lemonade out of lemons."

The Five C's of Success

While it's difficult to know a good soundbite until you hear one, successful ones can generally be defined by the five C's: They are clear, concise, conversational, catchy and colorful.

Clear. Every business has its own jargon, acronyms and abbreviations. People get so used to talking their special language on the job, they easily slip into it during an interview. You're most successful in getting soundbited if you put a "jargon-o-meter" on your mouth to monitor unclear terms. Even if the reporter understands what you're talking about, the readers or listeners probably won't.

Don't say, "We need to lower the marginal tax rate." Instead say, "We need to help people keep more of what they earn."

Concise. Thomas Jefferson once said, "The most valuable of all talents is never using two words when one will do." This is absolutely essential when you're aiming for a soundbite a reporter will use.

Don't say, "It is our full intention and plan to have a newer, more efficient operation in place in 30 days." Instead say, "We'll upgrade operations in the next month."

Probably the best soundbite I ever used came during an interview with a police captain talking about the dangers of his profession, despite the intensive training officers go through: "You can do everything right in this career and still lose."

Conversational. Talk the way you would normally talk to a friend or family member. Don't use big, complicated words when short, simple ones will do. Use contractions to make your language less formal.

Don't say, "We will utilize a plethora of examples and ideas to make this manuscript come alive for our readers." Say instead, "We'll use many examples and ideas to make our concepts come alive."

Chapter One

In the newsroom, we were most frustrated by police officers who regularly spoke in non-conversational language, "We apprehended the alleged perpetrator at 0100 hours as he was exiting the structure carrying a small appliance." How much better to hear something like, "We caught the suspect early this morning as he ran out of the store carrying a television."

Catchy. The catchier your words, the more likely they are to be used by the reporter, and the more likely they will be remembered by the audience. Try a reference to something familiar to your viewers or a play on words.

President Clinton used a catchy phrase to talk about the affirmative action program: "Mend it, don't end it."

In a turnabout, when I made my career change from television to speaking and consulting, I was interviewed by a newspaper reporter. At one point I told her, "I think I can shape a career that fits me, rather than me having to fit a career." As I said those words, I had the feeling that they sounded fairly quotable, something I would have used if I were in her shoes. Not only did she use the statement in her story, but it appeared as a "pull quote," in bold print.

Colorful. Paint a picture for your listeners. Use examples, vivid words, and emotion.

One of my favorite colorful soundbites came from Claire Sargent who was a candidate for the U.S. Senate running against a powerful male incumbent. A theme of her campaign was the importance of getting new perspectives in Washington by electing more women. Instead of the usual trite rhetoric, she found a more colorful, quotable way of making her point: "It's time we elected Senators with breasts," she said. "We've been electing *boobs* long enough."

What Gets Soundbited

An interviewee who has mastered the five C's is like a driver who knows the road. But the driver is always a complex human being, moved and motivated by intellect and emotions. How, you may ask, can intellect and emotions be made to best serve you during an interview that deals with 9 to 5 business matters?

Here are a handful of those specifics that in my years of reporting I found helped interviewees come across as knowledgeable and caring, regardless of the subject they were discussing.

Personal Experiences/Emotions. Talk about what you see, hear and feel or what others see, hear and feel.

When I interviewed a teacher about his school closing because of low enrollments, his answer reflected his emotions: "We're all reacting differently. It's like a death. For some the pain fades quickly. Others, like me, will be mourning this for a long time."

Chapter One

A developer reacted like this to a city's plan to enact an 18-month moratorium on new building: "I'm in total shock. I feel like I woke up with a bomb in my front yard."

Specific Examples. Bring the ideas down to a level your audience can relate to by using specific examples.

House Speaker Newt Gingrich avoided generalizations when he discussed the problems we're having in society today: "You cannot maintain civilization with 12-year-olds having children, with 13-years-olds killing each other, with 17-year-olds dying of AIDS, with 18-year-olds getting diplomas they can't even read."

A leasing agent tried to explain why it was taking so long to fill a large space in an upscale shopping mall after a major tenant moved out. "We're not selling a pencil. Not many retailers are large enough to use a space like that."

An attorney who was asked how much money he had made on a land deal didn't want to give actual amounts. He used other specifics instead: "I make more than the governor, but less than Michael Jordan." What is so compelling about this example is not only the figure of Michael Jordan's salary but also the visual image in our minds of his graceful movements to the basket time after time.

Contemporary References. These relate to what's happening in popular culture. Walter Mondale's comment, "Where's the beef?" during a debate with President Ronald Reagan was a take-off on a popular TV commercial for Wendy's restaurants.

When discussing the misuse of scanners at grocery stores and how customers are unknowingly being overcharged, a consumer advocate used a reference to a popular, long-running TV show: "This game is called 'The Price is Wrong' — and consumers are the losers."

Analogies. Analogies help your audience understand and visualize what you're talking about because they compare generalized concepts with more specific ideas people can relate to.

Ross Perot used this visual analogy to explain how the United States is slipping from economic leadership: "We're like an old heavyweight fighter with a 50-inch waist looking in the mirror and saying 'I am still the greatest.' We're sitting around soft and the Japanese are eating our lunch."

During the O.J. Simpson trial, Court TV accidentally showed the face of a juror during its coverage. Defense attorney F. Lee Bailey expressed his feelings about irresponsible producers: "If they'd been flying a plane, they'd have killed 300 people."

Clichés. Even clichés, which we normally try to avoid in our writing, can be intriguing to reporters because they make difficult concepts easy to understand. Examples include: "It's either feast

Chapter One

or famine when you're trying to start your own business," and, "We're caught between a rock and a hard place in making this decision."

One-Liners. During the gloom of the depression, Franklin Delano Roosevelt reached back to his reading of Thoreau for this enduring one-liner, "The only thing we have to fear is fear itself."

Knowing his soundbite would be replayed again and again throughout future decades, Neil Armstrong planned carefully his words upon being the first human to walk on the moon — "One small step for man, one giant leap for mankind."

Good one-liners are quick and easy to remember. That's why George Bush purposefully used his often repeated "Read my lips, no new taxes" during the presidential campaign. Unfortunately, later, after he was elected and ended up raising taxes, he wished people would forget his memorable one-liner. They didn't.

Absolutes. Is your program the "first" or the "best?" Is a policy the "worst" or the "most dangerous?" Is there something you will "never" do? If you can say it without stretching the truth, and could live with the consequences if some day proved wrong, the media will likely quote you.

Bob Mays talked to reporters about the daughter he was raising, who had been switched at birth, and his fight to keep her from her natural parents. Of the Twig family he said: "I wouldn't care if they traced her heritage to a cabbage patch, she's mine. I'm her father. I always have been and I always will be."

Proportional Numbers. When you must use statistics, make them easy to understand. Round off numbers and use percentages.

Rather than saying, "48 people attended the meeting," say "Nearly 50 people attended."

Instead of saying, "80 out of 100 people are in favor of the proposition," say "80 percent of people favor the proposition" or "four out of five people favor it."

Quote the Opposition. Has the opposition ever agreed with you or praised you? Use their quote to make what you say quotable.

Has the opposition ever said anything you can use to your advantage? Republicans jumped with glee when President Clinton said this during a speech to business leaders: "You think I raised your taxes too much. It might surprise you to know I think I raised them too much, too."

Humor. Humor can be a powerful communication weapon. But when practiced inappropriately, it can also blow up in your face. Don't use gallows humor which may be funny as an inside joke with your co-workers but doesn't play well to a general audience.

Don't use racist, sexist or other politically incorrect humor. An executive of an NFL football team risked insulting every woman in the audi-

Chapter One

ence when he said this in response to a question about refurbishing an old stadium: "You can take an old broad and give her a facelift, good cosmetics and dye her hair, but she's still an old broad."

Self-deprecating humor is safer than attacking someone else. If you do make fun of someone else, make sure it's good-natured ribbing, or that the person isn't someone the audience looks at sympathetically.

During the Persian Gulf War, General Norman Schwartzkopf successfully made fun of his enemy's ability to lead Iraqi troops: "As far as Saddam Hussein being a great military strategist, he's neither a strategist, nor is he schooled in the operational art, nor is he a tactician, nor is he a general, nor is he a soldier. Other than that, he's a great military man."

Ross Perot didn't mind that he was quoted casting aspersions on General Motors while explaining why his partnership with the company didn't work: "I come from an environment where if you see a snake, you kill it. These guys see a snake, get a consultant on snakes, form a committee on snakes, think about it for a year, and by the time they do anything, there are snakes all over the factory."

Ronald Reagan used humor effectively to defuse the "age issue" while campaigning for President against Walter Mondale: "I won't make age an issue in this campaign. I promise not to exploit for political purposes my opponent's youth and inexperience."

Negligible Nibbles
vs.
Successful Soundbites

To get the feel for shaping successful soundbites, let's look at some more specific examples. Compare carefully *what might have been said* to *what actually was said,* — the negligible nibble to the successful soundbite. The negligible nibbles, although generally informing, are rambling and lifeless. The successful soundbites draw their strength from the five C's by being clear, concise, conversational, catchy and colorful.

In the following examples, the negligible nibble is what might have been said by a well-intentioned but less-than-skillful speaker. It is followed by what was actually said and quoted by reporters. In every instance, the speaker of each soundbite gave the reporter a message so compelling he or she delivered it as quotable news.

Politicians

Former Senator Barry Goldwater taking about letting gays join the military.

Negligible nibble:
"Sexual orientation doesn't determine whether or not someone is a good soldier."

Chapter One

Soundbite:
"I don't care if a soldier is straight as long as he can _shoot_ straight."

Senator Dennis DeConcini defending the air interdiction program to stop drug traffickers from flying over the U.S./Mexico border, a program opponents claim is ineffective.

Negligible nibble:
"It's difficult to keep records on how many people get apprehended because that's not the major goal of the air interdiction program. Its primary strength is deterring drug traffickers so they won't try to fly across the border with their drugs."

Soundbite:
"Let's say you put a fence around a cabbage patch and the rabbits can't get in to eat the cabbage. Then you say, 'Why put the fence up? Nobody's eating any cabbage?' That's the point. The air interdiction deters people from flying across, so you're not going to catch them."

President George Bush talking about the Berlin wall before it fell.

Negligible nibble:
"The wall has obviously been a failure all these years. We are doing everything we can to make sure that it comes down."

SoundBites

Soundbite:
"That wall stands as a monument to the failure of Communism. It must come down."

A gubernatorial candidate reacting to news that the polls showed him losing.

Negligible nibble:
"I don't think you can believe polls. They are often wrong and don't accurately project what people are really thinking or how they will end up voting."

Soundbite:
"Pollsters make astrologers look credible."

Public Officials

An investigator talking about the explosion over Lockerbie, Scotland of a Pan Am flight, enroute from London to New York, explained why the bomb had not been detected by metal detectors.

Negligible nibble:
"This was a very sophisticated plastic explosive which was composed of very little metal."

Soundbite:
"There was less metal in that plastic explosive than in the fly on my pants."

Chapter One

A city mayor talking about reducing juvenile crime.

Negligible nibble:
"The crime problem is not easily solved with one quick remedy. It has a variety of causes and therefore we need to install a variety of solutions to attack the problem. We need preventative measures that stop children from getting into trouble to begin with, and we need tougher enforcement once they do commit crimes."

Soundbite:
"My experience working on the crime problem tells me you have to apply a hammer and a hug. The hug side are programs like preschool for at-risk kids. The hammer side are things like making sure that when juveniles commit serious crimes they're tried as adults."

O.J. Simpson's trial prosecutor Marcia Clark talking about how the media sensationalize things.

Negligible nibble:
"The media like to blow things out of proportion. They find out one small bit of information and pretty soon they make assumptions and write stories which just aren't true."

Soundbite:
"The media take one kernel of truth and blow it up into a huge bowl of popcorn."

SoundBites

Business People

A spokesman for a new upscale discount department store just opening its first location in the area.

Negligible nibble:
"Our store concept is to give our customers good selection, good prices in a convenient location."

Soundbite:
"We combine the taste level of Bloomingdale's with the convenience of a 7-Eleven and the prices of a Wal-Mart."

The human relations person for a manufacturing company talking about negotiations with its union on a new contract:

Negligible nibble:
"We expect to come to an agreement soon as we continue to bargain in good faith with the union management and our employees. The union is concerned about contracting for six years this time rather than the three years as we've done in the past. We think there are many benefits of the longer contract. One is that employees get more job security. For our customers, it means they'll get uninterrupted supplies, and for the company, it means we can do strategic planning for a longer period of time in the future."

Chapter One

Soundbite:
**The longer contract is good for everyone.
It gives our employees job security, it
assures our customers of interrupted
supplies, and it gives the company a
chance to plan ahead for a longer period."**

A utility company executive talking about why his
company built an energy-efficient and environ-
mentally-friendly showcase house:

Negligible nibble:
*"Our major goal is to showcase things that
people can use and apply when they build
their homes to make them more environmentally friendly while also saving energy."*

Soundbite:
**"Builders won't build it unless buyers
demand it. Buyers can't demand it unless
they know about it."**

An architect talking about how he designs homes
that blend into the environment.

Negligible nibble:
*"It's important that we architects reconcile our
clients' needs with those of the land that we're
building on to be able to meet the specific
conditions of the site."*

31

SoundBites

Soundbite:
"I listen closely to my clients, then listen to the land as well."

Citizens

A person from the opposition talking about why voters passed a tax increase to set up a mountain preserve in their city.

Negligible nibble:
"Voters were not aware that this proposal didn't live up to its claims. They were taken in by those who favored the tax increase."

Soundbite:
"This was a nice shiny package with environmental ribbons tied around it and people didn't bother to open it up and look inside."

An anti-smoking activist talking about how effective the tobacco companies have been in promoting their interests.

Negligible nibble:
"Compared to us, the tobacco companies have huge amounts of money to spend lobbying government and advertising their products around the world. This successful campaign of theirs is killing a lot of innocent people."

Chapter One

Soundbite:
"When you look at what they're doing and what we're doing, they are doing the better job. They're literally making a killing around the world."

A voter cautioning his fellow citizens about taking the election process seriously.

Negligible nibble:
"There is a movement in this country to throw out all the politicians in Washington right now. But we have to be careful. Not everyone running for office is better than what we already have."

Soundbite:
"We can throw the bums out, but we can throw the bums in, too, unless we watch what we're doing in the voting booth."

What *Not* to Do

Clear, concise, conversational, catchy and colorful soundbites can also get you into trouble when they carry another "C"— controversy — or an "S"— stupidity. Even though dressed fashionably with the five C's, controversial or plainly idiotic statements can get you quoted when you don't want to be. A reporter can't resist using a stupid or juicy statement, whether intended or unintentional, even though it makes you look bad.

SoundBites

George Bush's "Read my lips, no new taxes," mentioned earlier, and President Bill Clinton's comment about smoking marijuana, "I tried it once. I didn't like it. I don't even think I inhaled," definitely did damage to their speakers, as did the following painful examples . . .

Discussing a controversial policy on allowing employees to take county-owned cars home, a public official appeared stupid when he was simply being honest:

> *"We talked it over and that's what we came up with. We really have no rationale for it, to tell you the truth."*

A well-informed and thoughtful mining official, caught off guard when she answered the phone at home, was asked by a reporter about copper tailings which ran into a nearby creek, polluting it. Her reply was clear, concise, conversational, catchy, colorful and unintentionally disastrous:

> *"It's a nightmare, an absolute nightmare."*

General Stockdale, running for Vice President with Ross Perot, during a vice presidential debate gave reporters this gem of stupidity:

> *"What did you say? My hearing aid was turned off."*

Chapter One

A department store manager talking about Christmas sales was a little too blunt:

"Business stinks."

Former Arizona governor Evan Mecham commented about how much Japanese people like to play golf. Meaning to be clever, he came off as culturally insensitive, if not racist:

"Their eyes turn round when they see how many golf courses we have in Arizona."

Former President George Bush was given to speaking off the cuff. In praising the late band leader Lawrence Welk, he blurted out this reporter-pleasing boo boo:

"I'm all for Lawrence Welk. He's a wonderful man. He used to be, or was, or wherever he is now, bless him."

Secretary of State Alexander Haig, striding into the White House briefing room after President Reagan was wounded in a 1981 assassination attempt, thought he was establishing order at the national level. Instead, he shook up the nation with these words:

"As of now, I am in control here in the White House."

SoundBites

Defense Secretary Robert McNamara became himself an intellectual casualty when he spoke of deaths of Americans during the Vietnam War:

"The body count is at acceptable levels."

Senator Jesse Helms, talking about why federal spending on AIDS research should be reduced, revealed more bias than senatorial wisdom:

"It's a disease transmitted by people deliberately engaging in unnatural acts."

Senator Dennis DeConcini plainly misspoke while talking about the budget deficit:

"We're finally going to wrestle to the ground this giant orgasm that's out of control."
(Do you suppose he meant to say "organism?")

The best rule is never say anything on camera or to a reporter you wouldn't like to see on TV, read in the paper, or hear on the radio. Also, in answering a question, keep what you say in context. Don't leave a damaging phrase hanging out, inviting the reporter to lop it off, or use it without the rest of your thought. Here's an example of a mere pause that could have turned a reasonable statement into a political hot potato:

While Dick Cheney was Secretary of Defense, he talked to reporters about eliminating

Chapter One

Army reserve units across the country. There had been criticism that this would hurt communities economically by cutting jobs. Here's what Cheney said:

> **"We're not a social welfare agency. We're not an employment agency. We're not an agency that's operated on the basis of what makes sense (PAUSE) for some member of Congress back home in the district."**

Because of the pause, Cheney could have been quoted accurately but out of context:

> **"We're not an agency that's operated on the basis of what makes sense."**

Had he left out the pause, the reporter would have had to use the clear and cogent entire soundbite:

> **"We're not an agency that's operated on the basis of what makes sense for some member of Congress back home in the district."**

Chapter 2

Building Media Relationships

Time, working its inevitable changes, reveals this truth: Our world has become a global village in which communication is constant, almost instantaneous, and always crucial. Via newspapers, radio, television, and online computer services we speak our minds, declare our truths, conduct our business, and meet our common need to inform and be informed. Communication — it bears repeating — is crucial.

Elders remind us this has always been true — more or less. They cite those memorable fireside chats of President Franklin D. Roosevelt during the dark days of the Great Depression. Those chats, they say, saved a nation that had lost its way and restored our faith in ourselves, our government, our economic system. Others, perhaps more wary of media's awesome power, remind us of Adolph Hitler . . . how completely by his oratory he dominated and misled the German people, twisted and turned them and the world to earth-shattering war. Elders taking a kinder view of communication and history will cite Winston Churchill's oratory that countered Hitler's despotic messages and communicated to the free world those democratic ideas and ideals it could rally around.

Chapter Two

And who can forget one moment of powerful communication that gives me goose bumps each time I see and hear it replayed on television? Martin Luther King stirred the nation with his "I Have a Dream" speech delivered to 200,000 people in Washington DC on August 28, 1963. Profoundly influenced by The Bible and biblical phrasing, as was Abraham Lincoln before him, King used the media throughout his life to convert public sentiment to reality. What he did, you and I must marvel at, but what he did we too can practice in our own way if we understand successful communication and accept it as the challenge it is.

Why Deal with the Media?

Once in grade school, when I was angry with my best friend Joannie because she wouldn't do what I wanted her to do, my grandmother told me, "Be nice to her, Kathy. You always catch more bees with honey than with vinegar." Though I didn't fully understand it then, I've heard and applied that old adage, or versions of it, many times since. During my days as a reporter, I came to respect companies and organizations that were smart enough to practice their equivalent of Grandma's wisdom.

I have thought long and hard about others who would have benefited from that wise woman's counsel. I have in mind the two grocery store chains I called to help with a story on "Grocery Store Wars" in my area, one of the most competitive grocery markets in the country. I had difficulty with Grocery Chain A, one of the major players in town. When I finally got through to an executive there, she told me they had a policy they followed without exception — they never talked to the news media under any circumstances.

"Could I," I asked, "at least bring a camera into one of the stores to get some pictures?"

"Absolutely not," she said. "We never allow cameras in the stores." I was surprised — and frankly a little miffed — that they were turning away the benefits of free publicity.

The next company I tried, Grocery Chain B, had a completely different attitude. "We'd love to help you," the PR executive said. "How soon and at which store can we expect you and your photographer?" Then she added, "If you'd like, we can set up an area for you to interview some of our customers. And of course the store manager will be glad to talk to you."

Need I say, I did the story with soundbites and plenty of video from Grocery Chain B. That story ran a month or so before Thanksgiving. Not long after, I was assigned to do our regular Thanksgiving story on the price of turkeys and how grocery stores use them as loss leaders. Guess which grocery chain I called? I knew Grocery Chain B would go out of their way to make theirs a story I would want to put on TV. The finished report ended up being a minute and a half long — what actually turned out to be a minute and a half of free advertising for them on the late news! Although I never checked the exact details, I'm sure Grocery Chain B sold a lot of turkeys and fixin's that year.

But there's another chapter to this story. The first grocery chain, the one with the closed-door media policy, faced a communication crisis a few months later. Two of its employees chased a customer they suspected had passed a bad check. Pursuing him into the parking lot, they attempted to apprehend him. During the scuffle, the customer was knocked to the ground and died of his injuries.

The media descended on Grocery Chain A like vultures. The desperate CEO held a news conference trying to explain what had happened and how the investigation would proceed. By the time the reporters got through with him, however, the carcass of Grocery Chain A was all but picked clean.

If the same crisis had happened to Grocery Chain B, the one with the open-door policy, I believe they would have been covered by a kinder, gentler media. The reporters would still have done their job; they would have asked tough questions about a terribly tragic incident. But they would have done so based upon previous exchanges with the company's representatives. Like most of us, reporters are likely to give people they know and respect the benefit of the doubt. Ear-

SoundBites

lier rapport building with the media would have eased communication in this crisis.

Whether the story is good news or bad, think of the media not as an obstacle but as an opportunity to tell your side of the story. Never neglect an opportunity to convey what you feel and what you know. The media door swings both ways. If you don't open your door to reporters during controversial times or on bad news days, they won't open theirs when you ask them to cover good news stories, the ones that serve your interest.

And that coverage can definitely help you. Free publicity is often better than paid advertising because you gain credibility from an impartial third-party endorsement. There are no limits on communication except your ingenuity and creative thinking. You can promote a new product, push for legislation that benefits your industry, or counter dangerous claims made by others.

Ask any successful author how many books he or she sells when a favorable story appears in the media. Ask any charity how much more money pours in when the media champion its cause. When the call goes out over radio, TV and newspapers that blood supplies are low, donations at local blood banks increase dramatically. And, of course, successful politicians thrive on media coverage and will do almost anything to make the evening news.

But you and I, whatever our roles, can benefit as well. I once did a feature story on a chimney sweep who recommended that, to prevent fires, people get their chimneys cleaned every year before using their fireplaces. The story had a certain Mary Poppins simplicity and grandeur, including the sweep in old English top hat wielding his magic broom as though it were a baton. Although I don't remember the specific soundbites, I thought at the time that they were clever and concise. That story ran on the 6 p.m. news. The next day, the chimney sweep received 21 calls from potential customers.

Relationship building with the media may begin with the CEO or PR director. But it's incumbent on your entire organization to let the media know you are open and accessible. The relationships you've worked so hard to build can be ruined in seconds by the phone operator who curtly tells a reporter no one is available, or the uninformed security guard who rudely puts his hand in the camera when a photographer arrives at the plant gate. Everyone in your organization who may come in contact with a reporter should be media savvy. This can be accomplished through training or via pointers printed in your company newsletter.

Keeping the lines of communication open is like putting money in the bank for a rainy day. When a crisis occurs, you can collect on the goodwill you've built over months and years. Good rapport with the media doesn't guarantee positive coverage, but it makes it more likely you'll be treated fairly.

SoundBites

To summarize, there can be great benefits in working with the media. Here are some:

- *You can get free publicity. (Endorsement by a reporter often has more credibility than paid advertising.)*
- *You can correct wrong perceptions or information.*
- *You can tell your side of a controversy.*
- *You can influence the story. (Reporters will probably do the story with or without you, so it's best to participate.)*
- *You can be proactive rather than reactive if you initiate contact.*
- *You can build ongoing relationships with reporters. (These relationships will benefit you when the world smiles on you and are absolutely essential in managing a crisis.)*

These are the risks to consider when you open yourself to the media:

- *The story may turn out to be negative or unfair.*
But that will likely happen if you *don't* talk to reporters. By agreeing to an interview, you have a chance to more favorably influence their slant on the story.

- *The story may be inaccurate.*
You can limit inaccuracies by expressing your message clearly. You can also con-

firm that the reporter precisely under-stands your version of the story.

● *The story may misquote you.*
There's no guarantee against being mis-quoted. Still, you can limit the possibility by following the five C's defined in the pre-vious chapter.

● *The story may open up vulnerable ar-eas of inquiry.*
Prepare fully for the interview. Be ready to answer questions about any skeletons you have in the closet. Difficult issues may not come up, but you'll feel better know-ing you're prepared to handle them.

● *The reporter developing the story may take a lot of your time.*
Don't let a reporter make unrealistic de-mands on your time. Establish a time limit such as, "I have a half hour to talk to you." And do base the amount of time on the value of the proposed interview. How much is it worth to get out your message on the evening news or to have your business featured in the morning paper? Probably plenty. Remember this: Any time you spend with a reporter can build an ongo-ing media relationship with potential future benefits.

SoundBites

Anatomy of a Reporter

Building relationships with the media isn't much different from building relationships with co-workers, family or friends. To be successful, you must understand who you are, whom you are dealing with, and what they need and want. Reporters sometimes seem like people from a different culture who speak another language. It's tempting to think of the media as a monolithic being, but each reporter has his or her own likes and dislikes. You need to know as much as you can about every reporter you deal with.

Here are some background facts to consider in your interactions with reporters:

On Deadline. Deadlines guide the way reporters operate. They have to get the story fast, get it right, and make it interesting so the audience doesn't change the channel or decide not to buy the paper. To foster a successful relationship with them you must honor their deadlines. Don't ignore phone calls. Return all calls as soon as possible, even if you don't have the information they request or cannot take part in the interview they propose. Advise everyone in your operation that reporters' inquiries deserve high priority dictated by deadlines.

Contrary to what most people think, reporters don't have a lot of time to develop a story. Your receptivity acknowledges the deadlines under which they labor. They rarely have time to

tour your plant, read your 100-page annual report, or do lengthy research. Good reporters are
quick studies. Talking to you *is* their homework.
It's to your advantage, then, to help them obtain
the information they need. By assisting them, you
can advance the story you want told.

Limited time and space, as well as tight
deadlines prevent even an able reporter from telling the "whole" of any story. Each report is only a
limited look at an event or issue. The more involved you become in the story early on, the more
you can influence how it turns out.

Generalists. Understand that most reporters,
especially those on TV and radio, are generalists. Today they cover you and your company,
tomorrow they do a story on interest rates, the
next day they report on hot air ballooning. Most
of them are bright and dedicated workers, but
even the best of them may be relatively unknowl-
edgeable about your particular subject or issue.

Beat reporters and those at trade publications who cover your subject regularly will be more
informed than general news reporters. Still, they
lack your depth of knowledge and you may have
to educate them about your issues without talking down to them.

The best communication, though, sets
some limits. Only tell reporters what they need
to know. On occasion as an interviewer I asked
what time it was, to which the person explained
in minutes verging on hours how a clock works.

SoundBites

Such over-communication confuses the reporter and the issue. The story that gets told becomes fuzzy and inaccurate.

Suspicious. A joke overheard in the newsroom: "If reporters smell a rose, they look for a coffin." That's a light-hearted way of saying that journalists distrust just about everybody — in particular, people in power, big business and government. Sometimes called "the Watergate effect," this has been especially true since President Richard Nixon's resignation and the publicity given to the investigative reporting by Woodward and Bernstein at the *Washington Post*

The longer they're on the job, the more reporters have reason to become cynical and perhaps negative. Like police officers, they see a lot of the seamy side of life. They've been misled and lied to. Reporters assume you're only telling them part of the story, the positive part. That's why they may seem hostile when talking to you. As one reporter friend told me, "Kathy, we have to pick up the rock to see what's underneath."

In working with reporters, you must take their negativity in stride. Accept it, then do all you can to persuade them to your point of view. Facts and information are on your side and you should convey them without exaggeration or, even worse, lying. Cultivate credibility as a habit, as a virtue. Should you or anyone in your organization lose reporters' trust, it's difficult to get it back.

Chapter Two

Tenacious. Once reporters get hold of a good story, they hang on like a dog with a juicy bone. The more roadblocks you put in their way, the more determined they'll be to get the information. If you won't talk, they'll find someone who will — the disgruntled employee you fired last week or the neighbor across the street who has always distrusted your company.

I remember a news story very much to this point, the case of a nursing home which had two workers accused of abusing patients. Administrators, fearful of having to answer difficult questions, refused to talk to the news media. For what they thought were good reasons, they also refused to let cameras on the premises. A determined TV reporter and photographer waited outside the nursing home, on public property at the edge of the parking lot. As family members left after visiting their relatives who were patients, the crew got them to comment *on camera* with this loaded question, "How do you feel about workers here abusing patients?" Their answers, without exception, were extremely negative, charged with emotion, and TV viewers could not help but judge the nursing home harshly. How much better it would have been had the nursing home administrators faced the crisis openly, and used their interview as an opportunity to make the best of a bad circumstance.

Reporters thrive on facts; they pursue them with vigor. That's why you can benefit by being cooperative and forthright, by using your interview to make sure your story is covered fairly. Nothing shows better in the media than the naked truth.

Rude/Pushy. Reporters are paid to be curious, not polite. If you know where they're coming from, you can readily adapt, even to the point of being generous to meet their needs. Politeness and accommodation, the niceties you and I practice every day in the business world, will win the day with the news media, as with the public. Even if reporters appear rude and pushy, showing no respect for you or anyone in your organization including the CEO, you must not take it personally. Accept it as just part of their job and adjust to it with grace.

Keep in mind that reporters are paid to ask questions which may be difficult or offensive. They pound down the media highway as though they had blinders on. Their only goal: get the story no matter what. Sometimes it is difficult to stay calm in the face of their rudeness.

Bored. Odd as it sounds, journalism, even the television version, is like most professions. To those who practice it, it isn't as glamorous as it looks to outsiders. Reporters, even the best of them, find themselves doing what seems a similar story over and over. Responding to the same drives you and I have for freshness and vitality, they try to work new angles, create novel and engaging stories. What appears to be exaggeration and sensationalizing, may be more precisely a reporter's avoidance of boredom, and an effort to sell his editor on the value of a story. By seeking to entertain themselves and their audiences, reporters are doing their best to assure that their lives add up in the scale of human values.

Steeped in Their Own Values. Reporters look at the world from a different perspective than do most of us. Their bottom line is to generate interest and dramatize an issue, not color it rosy for a particular person or organization. Caught up in their own values, reporters appear, and may indeed be, self-righteous. They believe it's incumbent upon them to protect the public from business people, politicians, bureaucrats, almost any person whose power base is different from theirs. They naturally tend to favor the one they consider the victim or the "little guy." Knowing this bent, if not bias, you and your organization can negate the tendency of reporters to set up a "David vs. Goliath" type story.

Professionals. Most people in media are well-educated professionals. Simply stated, they consider it their job to inform the public. In the United States, they rightly view themselves as empowered and protected by the First Amendment to the Constitution. In working with them, you will insult their professionalism if you ask to review a story before publication. Such a request raises the red flag of censorship.

SoundBites

To avoid having that red flag pop up in a reporter's head, you may suggest that he or she feel free to call you back for clarification or to verify quotes. But never demand that they do so. You will only alienate yourself from the reporter and perhaps damage greatly your relationship with the media. If your dealings with reporters sustain their professionalism, you will be practicing your own professionalism at its best.

Know the Newsroom

Most consumers of news are relatively uninformed about the newsroom and its role in communication. To name it as the inner sanctum of media is not to overstate its function. Whether we are speaking of television, newspapers, radio, or wire services, the newsroom is where the action is generated and where much of what goes out to the public takes its shape. Only the most recent development of media, online computer services, exists without this central nerve center. To understand the newsroom's role is to gain a leg up on using its services.

In many ways, each of the four — television, newspapers, radio and wire services — operates by roughly the same personnel structure and chain of command. Although job titles and descriptions may vary, the newsroom always functions on the premise of deciding what's important to cover, assigning those stories, gather-

52

Chapter Two

ing the pertinent information and facts, evaluating their worth, ordering stories according to their value, and dispensing them in the most engaging way.

Television. The special niche in communication occupied by television turns on two axes: visuals and sound. A television newsroom's first concern is with visuals, for visuals determine what gets covered. Without visuals, there is no television story. Sound, as important as it is, is usually subordinate to the visuals to which it applies. The personnel who are most important in determining the "look" of the newscasts are the News Director, Producers, Assignment Editors, Anchors, Reporters and Photographers.

News Director. The News Director is in charge of running the news department and reports to the station General Manager. The larger the TV market, the farther away the News Director is from day-to-day news operations. While he or she helps determine what stories are covered and how, this is usually not the person to contact about placing stories.

However, if you are unhappy about a particular story that included you or your company, and you have not been able to get satisfaction from the reporter who did it, you can take your case to the News Director. Likewise, this is the person to approach if you have compliments or complaints about news coverage.

SoundBites

Producers. Each news program has a Producer who is responsible for choosing what stories will go into the show, their length and format, and their sequence. The Producer (with the help of an Assistant Producer at larger stations) writes any stories not covered by individual reporters. This includes rewriting wire copy and writing "teases" before the commercials that try to convince the audience to stay tuned.

Reporters often write the lead-ins to their stories (read on-air by the anchors), but the Producer may rewrite them to punch them up or help them tie in better with another story.

The Producer also has time-keeping responsibilities during the show. He or she must make sure the program ends exactly when it is scheduled to. This may mean deciding to drop stories or cut time from the weather or sports segments.

If the news show includes live guests, the Producer books them and briefs the hosts or anchors. Programs like *Oprah*, *The Today Show*, and *Nightline* have several producers who pre-interview potential guests and book them.

Assignment Editors. The Assignment Editor determines what stories are covered, when they are covered, and by whom. He or she is the most important person to know in any TV newsroom. This is the person to whom you send news releases or call about story placements.

Unfortunately for those of you trying to

Chapter Two

place a story, (or "pitch a story" in public relations jargon), Assignment Editors are harried people. They're the traffic controllers of the newsroom. As the news day progresses, they must constantly react to changes and problems. A crew must be diverted to a fire or accident. A story the Producers were counting on falls through. A camera or vehicle breaks down. The crew can't find the location for its noon live shot. Then, toward the end of each day, the Assignment Editor must plan and schedule stories for the next day.

If you call an Assignment Editor, keep your message short and to the point.

Anchors. Anchor people are the "stars" of the newscast. In their "shining," they become identified with the show. Before going on air, they read over and sometimes revise what has been written by Producers and Reporters. On air, they read copy stories, voice-overs, lead-ins to Reporters' stories, and teases. They usually introduce the Weathercaster and Sportscaster.

Anchors' duties and hours vary widely, depending on what newscast they do and what kind of deal they've struck with the station. Some anchors don't research or write stories. They are simply "readers," who rely on Producers and Reporters to do all the behind the scenes work. Other Anchors are actively involved in helping Producers put the show together and going out in the field to research and write special stories.

Anchors sometimes choose what stories

to cover in their newscasts and they may at least influence what news gets covered. If you have a story that might interest an Anchor, consider contacting him or her directly.

Reporters. Reporters are the on-air talent who put together stories they've gathered in the field. They get information, interview people on camera, write the story and supervise its editing.

Most Reporters are "general assignment," which means they cover anything and everything, usually by assignment from the Assignment Editor. But general assignment Reporters are also encouraged to develop their own story ideas. Beat Reporters or Special Assignment Reporters have specified areas to cover, such as consumer news, features, health or investigative. They regularly come up with their own story ideas.

If you have established a relationship with a certain Reporter or know from watching the news that someone has a particular interest, you can sometimes pitch a story idea to him or her directly. Should you approach both a station's Reporter and Assignment Editor with the same idea, tell each that you've contacted the other.

Should you wish to complain about a given story, it's highly desirable to call the Reporter who did the story and give him or her first opportunity to respond to your complaint. Not only is it the courteous thing to do, but it will often result in establishing rapport, especially when the facts are on your side. After talking to the Reporter, if you still feel your complaint has not been addressed, call the News Director.

Photographers. I was amazed how many times the people I interviewed ignored the photographer, acting as if he or she wasn't there. Be nice to photographers — They're the ones who determine how you look! They can also influence how the Reporter covers your story and what the visuals turn out to be.

Photographers are sometimes sent to cover a story without a Reporter. Later, a Producer or Reporter will call for information to go with the video shot by the Photographer. When Reporters and Photographers cover a story together, the Reporter is usually in charge, but most crews work together as a team.

At some stations, Photographers may edit their own stories with guidance from Reporters and Producers. At other stations Photographers turn their video over to Editors who are in charge of editing all videotape that appears in the news programs. The principle to keep in mind is simply this: photographers are not only skilled artists with visuals, but also may know more about the story than the reporter they are working with.

Newspapers. Newspapers are contemporary media's oldest offspring. Long have they shaped our notions of news. In this age of computers and improved visuals, they have taken on a changed face predicated upon "make it visual" and "shorter

SoundBites

is better" philosophies. But the people who bring newspapers into being carry titles most of us remember from childhood, and these are the people you are likely to want to consult: Publisher, Managing Editor, City Editor/Metro Editor, Special Editors, Community Section Editors, Reporters, and Columnists.

Publisher. The Publisher is usually the CEO of the newspaper organization. He or she normally oversees the entire operation from advertising and classified ads to the news pages and editorials. On smaller papers, the Publisher may be owner and is likely to take an active role in every phase of news processing. On larger papers, the Publisher is less likely to be owner but quite likely to be responsible for the financial well-being of the newspaper. Most Publishers, in the tradition of journalism, are influential members and intellectual leaders in their communities.

Managing Editor. This person is the overall boss of the paper's news operations. The Managing Editor makes most production decisions and produces the newspaper as most readers know it. He or she is usually not the person to call to attempt to place stories, though he or she may be the person to call if you are unhappy about a story and do not get satisfaction from the Reporter.

City or Metro Editor. This person supervises and assigns Reporters and Photographers who are covering local and regional news. The City or Metro Editor directs Reporters who have specific beats such as City Hall or the Environment, and may designate general assignment Reporters to cover miscellaneous stories.

City or Metro Editors are usually open to news releases or calls on story ideas. Often, if they themselves do not respond to you, they will put you in touch with assistants on the City Desk or specific Reporters to whom you can pitch stories. Each newspaper has its own channels of news and news coverage, and an inquiry will enable you to find the best channel for your purposes.

Other Editors. Many of the larger papers have bestowed the title of Editor on the person in charge of specific sections. In the trade, it is said there is now an "Editor for Anything and an Editor for Everything," all of whom report to the Managing Editor. Editors that you may have occasion to contact include the Features Editor (in charge of special features and lifestyle or entertainment stories), the Business Editor (in charge of the Business Pages), Food Editor (in charge of the Food Section), Sports Editor (in charge of the Sports Pages), Photo Editor (in charge of the photo staff), and Calendar Editor (in charge of publicizing upcoming events and activities).

Community Section Editor or Bureau Chief. Large newspapers sometimes establish satellite

SoundBites

offices, headed by Community Section Editors or Bureau Chiefs, so they can better cover outlying areas. These Editors usually supervise a small staff of reporters and photographers who look for stories that don't necessarily have broad appeal, but specifically touch their local community audiences in one geographic part of a metro area. These Editors normally expect to be approached with stories and news releases generated in their immediate locale.

Reporters. Most Reporters at larger papers have beats or areas of expertise such as City Government, Politics, Police, Education, Computers, Health, Entertainment, etc. They generate their own story ideas or are assigned by the City Editor. But there are also General News Reporters who cover a variety of stories. On smaller papers, Reporters are likely to cover a diversity of stories.

By following the bylines in your newspaper you can often determine which reporter covers what. In case you are uncertain, a call to the City Desk will usually get you the name of the right Reporter for your story or news release. If you direct a story to a given Reporter as well as the City Editor or a Section Editor, make sure you let each know of your action.

Columnist. Columnists write their own versions of the news by including their opinions in their stories. They are free to choose their topics, but must answer to the Managing Editor.

If you are familiar with specific Columnists and the kinds of things they write about, you can contact them directly to pitch an idea. Again, let them know if you've contacted anyone else at the paper.

Editorial Page/Opinion Page (Op-Ed Pages) Writer. The editorial page is the place where the newspaper's opinions appear, including editorial cartoons expressing the cartoonists' opinions. Syndicated columnists express their opinions here, too.

The editorial pages also contain readers' viewpoints through letters to the editor. A well-thought-out letter may be one way for you to express your views on a topic or respond to criticism. You also may have an opportunity to write an opinion piece for your newspaper. Call the editorial department to see if they use opinion pieces and, if so, what the guidelines are for acceptance.

Radio. An old radio announcer I once hobnobbed with liked to say, "Sound's our means, speech our measure, and you bring your own imagination to our party." His insightful pronouncement, uttered in foghorn base, still rings in my ears today.

In 1920, the first radio station, KDKA, went on the air in Pittsburgh, Pennsylvania. Long before television, radio was the modern day "camp-

SoundBites

fire" families gathered round in those quiet hours after supper. They brought their imagination to make the sounds and speech come alive in shows like "The Shadow," "The Lone Ranger," and "Dragnet." They laughed at Jack Benny and Edgar Bergen with Charlie McCarthy.

Many times during the last 75 years, the death of radio has been predicted. Early radio morticians promised it would die a natural death, or newspapers and magazines would rise up and kill it. Pundits of the 1940's saw TV as guarantor of radio's demise. But it lived on, bringing early rock and roll music to the masses. More current predicted death dealers to radio — Citizens Band radio, cellular phones, computers, the Internet — have come, and radio continues, even sounds off with a resurgence. Early in 1996, Congress passed landmark legislation that removes restrictions on the radio industry and may lead to an expanding role for radio, akin to the cable TV explosion.

Today, there are hundreds of radio stations in the United States, many of them specializing in music and some supporting a plethora of talk shows, both national and local, sustaining public debate on a variety of issues. True, many stations function with minimal or no news departments. In these stations, most of the newscast material comes from wire service information which is usually read over the air as originally written (called "rip and read" in the radio business). Other stations which specialize in all news

Chapter Two

and talk have a larger staff which gathers and writes news, as well as delivers it on the air. The most important staff members for your purposes include: The News Director, Reporters, Talk Show Hosts, and Producers. These people may be valued allies in promoting your agenda.

News Director. The News Director is in charge of the day-to-day operations of the news department. He or she does the hiring and firing of news personnel, as well as deciding what stories Reporters will cover.

    The News Director usually is an on-air talent in addition to having management duties. At very small stations, he or she may wear other hats such as Program Director or Promotion Director. You can send the News Director news releases or call with information about a story — they're your best point of contact in radio news.

Reporters. Reporters gather news, write newscasts and do the on-air live broadcasts. They go out into the field to attend news conferences or report on spot news live from the scene. Reporters also record phone interviews with news sources to edit for broadcast. You can contact radio Reporters directly about placing stories.

Talk Show Hosts. Talk Show Hosts run their own shows. With their Producers' help, they choose topics and guests, and are free to express their own opinions. You can contact Talk

SoundBites

Show Hosts directly, but it's probably easier to get in touch with their Producer.

Producers. At large radio stations, Producers may help to write the news broadcasts that air regularly. At small stations, the reporters themselves write the newscasts. Producers book guests for talk shows and, generally speaking, every radio talk show has a key, behind-the-scenes producer who is the person to approach with your ideas.

Wire Services. While people outside of the news business don't think much about wire services, they have widespread influence on what is written and reported by newspapers, TV and radio. Almost every news outlet in the country subscribes to some kind of wire service. The larger services, like Associated Press (AP), have national offices which research and write national and international news stories to send to customers across the entire country. If your story is of national importance, the General Desk at AP headquarters in New York City will be your point of contact. Wire services also have regional or state offices called "correspondencies" or "bureaus" which report on local news sent to customers within their geographic area. These are some of the people you may wish to contact at regional offices.

Chapter Two

Bureau Chief. The Bureau Chief runs both the business side and the editorial side of the regional office. That means he or she tries to get new customers to subscribe to the wire service while also working to keep the old ones happy. This person is ultimately responsible for everything that goes out on the wire from his or her office but, depending on the size of the bureau, may not have much hands-on influence. In smaller bureaus, the Chief may actually do some writing.

It is often wise to send or FAX your news releases to the Bureau Chief simply because he or she is too busy to accept phone calls. In larger bureaus, the Chief will pass your releases on to the appropriate people.

News Editor. This person does have hands-on responsibility for what goes out on the wire for newspapers. He or she may also have responsibility for what goes out to television and radio stations if there is no Broadcast Editor at the Bureau. The News Editor plans and directs coverage, and assigns stories to individual writers and photographers. Often the News Editor will write some of the stories put on the wire. In most cases, this is the best person to send news releases to at a wire service.

Broadcast Editor. Some bureaus may have a separate Broadcast Editor responsible for planning and directing coverage for everything that goes on the wire for television and radio stations.

SoundBites

For stories specifically targeting electronic media, you can send news releases to this person.

Daybook. Every state AP wire service puts out a daily "AP Daybook" which lists events that are happening on that particular day that may be of interest to reporters. This is an important place for you to elicit coverage for important events you have coming up — news conferences, public hearings, speeches, a march on the Capitol, etc. The Daybook items should include name and phone number.

The national wire has a segment called the Planner, which is the national version of the Daybook. Larger cities such as New York, Los Angeles, and Washington DC have their own local Daybooks.

Never Say "No Comment"

My dear grandmother who taught me to be affirmative rather than negative was not a "one-note Nellie." She often spoke of the fine line between what to do and what not to do. Were she at my side at this moment, I'm sure she'd say, "Kathy, you've told what to do to build successful media relationships. Now, for goodness sake, say what *not* to do."

The first thing not to do if you wish to open the doors to successful media communication and keep them open, is never say "no comment" to a

Chapter Two

reporter. Forget all the movies and TV shows that portray just the opposite. You know the scene where the Senator hurries out of the building pursued by TV cameras and reporters sticking microphones in his face while yelling questions. Suddenly he turns and shouts "NO COMMENT," then continues rushing toward the waiting car. If you say those two words, you'll sound guilty — like you have something to hide. That's how "no comment" is interpreted by both the media and the public.

We've seen from earlier examples that a story will not go away just because you choose not to talk. If you don't cooperate, the reporter will talk to your customers or competitors, a disgruntled employee, or the witness who just happened to be passing by. They'll come to their own conclusions without you. It's much better for you to have a presence in the story.

If you give the impression of being open and honest by offering some kind of comment, reporters and the public are more likely to trust you. You have kept open the possibility of a relationship. If you can't say a lot about the topic, you can always say something. Even explaining why you can't talk is better than stonewalling. And you can use the opportunity to turn a potential negative story into a positive one.

Let's look at several examples from my own experience. One of my clients was general manager of a mine where a cave-in killed several workers. Reporters called immediately after the accident happened. No one was sure yet of all the details. It was tempting to say "no comment." Instead, the mine manager expressed empathy about the accident. He said it was a horrible tragedy for the miners' families and friends. He told reporters he didn't know how the accident had happened, but that the investigation was already underway. Then he talked about the things he did know: the concern the company had for its workers and the mine's excellent safety record. The resulting newspaper and television reports gave both sides of the story, and the mining company came across as compassionate instead of uncaring.

Another client in a fast-growing business was asked by reporters about company sales figures. Again, she avoided "no comment" and kept the lines of communication open by explaining to reporters that she couldn't talk about specifics that would give her competitors valuable information. She went on to speak in positive terms about the company's success as a result of its unique concept and concern for customers. She gave the reporters something they could use and they continue to contact her regularly for information.

Often reporters call to ask about employee firings and reprimands or other things you can't discuss because of privacy issues. Instead of saying "no comment," you could say something like: "We don't want to violate our employees' rights to privacy so we can't release specific information about this case. I can tell you in general that if employees receive three complaints in their personnel file in a one-year period, they are put on probation because we feel they aren't serving our customers." You come across as a real human being instead of an uncaring company bureaucrat who's stonewalling.

This doesn't mean you have to answer every question or discuss every issue a reporter calls you about. But when you don't want to or can't talk, tell reporters why. You'll be perceived as genuinely concerned and caring.

Consider these alternatives to "no comment."

"Our hearts go out to the friends and family of Mrs. Ellis. We're still investigating what happened and we won't know any specifics until we've gotten a final report."

"I don't think it's appropriate for me to talk about this issue with you because it's still in litigation and my attorney has advised me not to talk about it until after the trial is over."

"I'm not the best person to answer that. It's not my area of expertise. Let me find out who in the company is best to help you, and I'll have them call you."

"Because of our competition in the marketplace, we don't want to publicly reveal our revenue projections. We are on track this year to meet our goals."

When to Refuse an Interview

While you should almost always take advantage of a media opportunity, there are times to decline an interview request. If a reporter has continually treated you unfairly over a period of time and you haven't been able to resolve the conflict, then you may choose to not work again with that person. Talk to the editor or news director about assigning a different individual to cover your company. That still keeps the lines of communication open with the station or publication itself.

You don't want to freeze out the entire news organization, except in extreme cases. That's the proverbial cutting off your nose to spite your face. A client of mine once told me his company never talked to a certain TV station because their investigative reporter had done an unfair story on them. On further inquiry, it turned out the unfair story happened four years earlier. The reporter had long since moved on to another city and no one at the station remembered why this company wouldn't talk to them. Meanwhile my client had lost valuable opportunities to promote his issues on a major station in his community.

There may also be rare occasions when you should decline to talk because you can't confirm the reporter works for the media outlet he or she claims to represent. If you aren't familiar with the person who calls you for an interview and you doubt his or her truthfulness, it may be ap-

Chapter Two

propriate to call the station or publication to verify the assignment.

If one of the national TV news magazine shows like "60 Minutes," "Dateline NBC," "20/20," "American Journal," or "Inside Edition" calls for an interview, you have to consider your options carefully. While talking to them on camera could help you, it seems more likely to hurt you. Audi, the car maker, agreed to an interview with "60 Minutes" about the safety of one its models and felt violated by the finished story. Spokespersons claimed that editors left the company's best arguments on the cutting room floor, yet included in the story damaging statements from consumers and industry experts.

In another case, though, Coors Beer agreed to cooperate with "60 Minutes" and turned around a major controversy. Large blocks of people, including organized labor, were boycotting the company, claiming it treated its employees shabbily and abused their rights. To counter the claims, Coors owners opened all their records and their entire operation to Mike Wallace and his crew. They allowed him to talk to employees without restriction. It worked. Coors got more than ten minutes of positive coverage on "60 Minutes."

Throughout my career as a media trainer and crisis consultant, I have encouraged clients to be open and honest with the news media by agreeing to participate in their stories. Recently, though, I'm having second thoughts about that policy when it comes to the national TV news

71

magazines. Other experts also seem to agree it's unlikely that you'll come out ahead by doing an interview with one of the TV news magazines. When they are planning and researching a news story that will attract interest — and viewers — chances are they are approaching it with a negative bias. Despite the strength of your arguments, you may not be able to overcome perceptions of incompetence or wrongdoing. In most cases, you may be better off to simply send a written statement which they can use in the story. If you do decide to go on one of the national TV news magazines, I'd recommend extensive training and preparation.

Here's a caution, though, especially when working with local media: declining an interview for no apparent reason can land you in the doghouse with a reporter. He or she will also tell colleagues about your negative response. Even after that reporter changes publications or stations (possibly years down the road), your actions will be remembered. So think carefully before you decide to not cooperate with a reporter.

Chapter Two

To Be
"Off the Record"
or Not to Be

Some of my clients claim the best way to make friends with a reporter is to give him or her juicy information "off the record." I believe such performances only invite trouble.

"Off the record" means giving reporters information that they agree ahead of time not to use in the story. Government officials and others in Washington regularly use this tactic to leak information to reporters. They also depend on variations of "off the record" such as "not for attribution" — you can use the information but don't attribute it to me — and "on background" — you can use the information if you get it confirmed by another source.

For the average spokesperson, this game can be dangerous. Once reporters know juicy information, it's difficult for them not to use it somehow. They may spill the beans to a reporter at another publication or station who didn't agree to keep it off the record. They may at some point forget about their agreement. Your definition of "off the record" may be different from theirs. And there have been cases when a reporter has agreed that something is "off the record" but the editor overrides that decision and uses the information anyway.

Clients who play the off-the-record game

also claim they can help reporters better understand and cover a story by giving them inside information. There may be times when this risky tactic can have positive payoffs, but only if you're very careful. The only time to even attempt going off the record is when you have a long-standing relationship with a reporter built on trust. The reporter counts on you for ongoing stories, knowing that if he or she violates your confidence, you will be lost as a source. Make sure you have an agreement with the reporter your information is off the record *before* you divulge it. If you make a statement, then say, "By the way, that's off the record," it's probably too late.

Also be aware that if you go off the record often, odds are you'll eventually get burned. Reporters are not your ever loyal friends. The story comes first. One of my clients compared the reporter/source relationship to the one he shares with his pet snake. As much as they enjoy and respect each other, there's a good chance some day that snake will bite him.

Correcting Errors

After the interview is over and the story appears on the air or in the newspaper, what if you discover that the reporter didn't get it right? Your behavior in this situation will affect the way your relationship progresses not only with the reporter but also with his station or publication.

Chapter Two

If a story is inaccurate, you must follow up tactfully in order to keep the doors open for future stories.

It's inevitable that, under deadline pressure and with little in-depth knowledge about a subject, reporters will sometimes make mistakes. If that happens, stay calm, give feedback and be tolerant.

Complaining about a story — especially if you do it in anger or without thinking — can sometimes make matters worse. The issue may drag on longer rather than dying quickly. A one-day story could stretch to three days, guaranteeing that more people will read or hear about it. This quote, used often in Public Relations circles, says it best, "Don't get into an argument with someone who buys ink by the barrel." The same goes for reporters who buy their videotape by the case.

On the other hand, it's important to let reporters know you're watching closely and are expecting fair treatment. Effective feedback can help you maintain your relationship with the reporter and allow you to correct important information. Before you make a move to correct an error, think carefully about the following points.

Determine the importance of a mistake.

Is the mistake really as bad as you think? Get some objective viewpoints. You can't expect the news media to tell the whole truth as you see it. They don't have the time or space. Also, their perspective is different. They write what they think

SoundBites

is important after talking to you and other sources. The only way to have a story told exactly as you want it is to buy advertising or do a commercial.

Often those close to a story overreact. Perhaps a letter to the editor would be the best way to state your case. Make the letter rational and well-written. But never write a letter if it will further ignite a negative story.

Deal with the reporter first. Give the reporter the benefit of the doubt, and don't go immediately over his or her head. First talk directly to the person who interviewed you. Most reporters pride themselves on accuracy and are embarrassed when they make a mistake. Expect that they may naturally be defensive. Be positive and constructive. Use the contact as a chance to further educate the other person. As a last resort, contact the reporter's editor or news director.

Ask for Correction. If the error is significant enough to warrant a correction, politely ask for one. Explain why it's important. If the reporter won't consider it, you may have to call the editor or news director. Keep in mind one bit of my sage grandmother's counsel, "Kathy, dear, you can't unscramble an egg." The mistake you're so upset about may be corrected, but that correction will probably be buried somewhere in the back of the newspaper.

Also, be aware that it is easier to get a correction in the print media than in the electronic media. On television or radio you're not likely to get an on-air correction unless the mistake is significant or the station is afraid of getting sued. If they won't acknowledge a mistake on the air, you can ask for a short note or letter from them explaining the miscue. Tell them you'd like to have it on file in case of customer or public inquiry.

Avoid using the word "retraction." News people see a red flag when that word is mentioned. Instead, talk about a "correction."

Ask for Records Clarification. Even if the mistake doesn't warrant a correction in print or on the air, you should ask the reporter to make the correction in the computer or story file. Otherwise, as reporters research an issue or company for future stories by looking at what has been written before, the same incorrect information gets passed on from reporter to reporter and story to story.

Headline Complaints. It's important to be tolerant. If you're concerned about a headline, remember reporters don't write them. They turn in the story, but the Copy Editor decides what goes in bold letters above it. The same is true of the promotions and teases for TV and radio stories, things like "Coming up at six, XYZ Company dumps dangerous pollutants." The producer usually writes those after the reporter explains the story. Keep that in mind when you call to express concerns. Sometimes reporters are as unhappy about the teases and headlines as you are.

As long as you're willing to give news organizations feedback, consider some positive responses when they're warranted. Reporters are used to getting calls from people who don't like what they do. You can also call or write when you think they do an ou*tstanding* job and portray your story *accurately.* Don't thank them for the "positive" story. Thank them instead for a "fair and accurate" story.

Actual Headlines.

Sometimes what looks good on the copy editor's computer screen takes on a very different, unintended meaning when it gets to print.

IRAQI HEAD SEEKS ARMS

DEAD MAN FOUND IN CEMETERY

DEBRIS FOUND AROUND URANUS

HAZARDOUS WASTE BREAKFAST JUNE 6

SUSPECT IN BANK ROBBERY WAS EITHER MAN OR WOMAN

HIGH SPEED TRAIN COULD REACH VALLEY IN FIVE YEARS

PANTS BULGE PROVIDES NO BASIS FOR SEARCH

NUCLEAR WINTER MAY NOT BE SO BAD

35 APPLICANTS LINE UP FOR LORD'S JOB

WOMAN PREGNANT THANKS TO HER SISTER

Chapter Two

Ten Essentials of
Media Relationships

There are some final considerations when building relationships with the media. These are provided by Debra Gelbart, a former TV assignment editor and PR professional who is now an independent writer/editor and public relations specialist focusing on health care, insurance, service businesses and marketing communications issues.

1. Be Cooperative

Recognize that news people face constraints and expectations that most of us never dream of, and if you can say "yes" to a request for information or an interview, you are making their job that much less of a hassle. This also applies to special requests once an interview has been arranged and the news person steps into your world: find the electrical outlet needed; bring in the extra chair; take the crew to the unscheduled location within your facility. They will remember you for your responsiveness.

2. Be Accessible

Don't restrict your availability to the media to regular business hours. Give out your home phone number freely, and encourage reporters and editors to use it. If your organization is a 24-hour-a-day operation and someone else can

SoundBites

handle routine questions after hours, it may be perfectly acceptable as a matter of policy to direct those routine media calls to that person. But if a reporter does call you first, don't ask him to jump through hoops by saying, "Why don't you call so and so; I'm sure she can give you what you need." Get the answer yourself, relay it gracefully, and then suggest to the reporter that next time he or she can call the person on duty. Make sure the reporter has the appropriate phone number for that person. Let the reporter know that you are always available if a question cannot be answered by someone else satisfactorily. During business hours, try to return all phone calls from the media within an hour.

3. Be Direct

When you can't help a reporter, say so and explain why. Don't be defensive, don't sound pained and overburdened, and above all, don't display arrogance. You should be genuinely sorry that you can't help a reporter, because it is a missed opportunity for both of you. Learn to expect the modified requests that follow your apology: "Well, could you see if we could interview so and so instead?" Remember Rule Number One: Be Cooperative.

4. Be Fair

Don't give opportunities for in-demand interviews only to certain media outlets and not to others. If your CEO is suddenly thrust into the spotlight, for example, and agrees to just one block of time for an interview, don't offer that time only to the news organization screaming the loudest. In a similar circumstance, you can do one of two things: make it clear that the interview must be shared with any other interested media outlets (called "pool coverage") or hold a news conference. The second option is far less advantageous; unless there is news that you want to promote, it's very easy to lose control of the situation at a news conference. Ideally, you should give equal opportunity to all news organizations when there is something happening that interests them all. This does not preclude targeting or tailoring less obvious story suggestions for specific news organizations.

5. Be a Resource

Whenever possible, if you can't arrange an interview or answer a question for a reporter, suggest someone else — even among your competitors — who can. It's always better to end a conversation with a reporter by giving him another route to pursue instead of a dead end. And don't wait until he asks, "Can you think of anyone else who might know?" Volunteer, "I can't help you, but I think Bob Smith at the Trade Association may be able to. His number is . . ." Again, you will be remembered and respected.

SoundBites

6. Be an Authority

Learn all you can about your organization and industry: history, financial condition, goals, future, mission. And learn everything you can about how newsrooms, both print and broadcast, operate. Your goal should be to inform news people of important trends as well as converse knowledgeably with them about their business. When a television assignment editor asks you to arrange an "anchor interview" with one of your scientists, will you know what he's talking about? (It's a live interview with the news anchor while he's in the studio and you are in another location listening to him with an earpiece.)

7. Be an Educator

You need to educate two very different constituencies, your co-workers and media representatives, about each other. Hold workshops, informal meetings and media training seminars, if appropriate, to defuse distrust and misunderstanding. If your corporate culture embraces a working relationship with the media, you will be able to more successfully facilitate coverage for your organizations. If media representatives can learn about your company and your industry, they will be able to ask more intelligent questions. And, if they are familiar with the immovable stumbling blocks in your organization (such as top executives' jam-packed schedules), they will be more tolerant when you must say "no" to an interview request.

Chapter Two

8. Be an Advocate

It's sometimes tricky to walk that tightrope between two sets of clients — those within your organization and those in the media. Though one of your primary responsibilities is to present your organization favorably to the media, it is just as important to reinforce the value of the media to your organization. It's difficult to practice media relations successfully if you view news organizations as the "enemy" or if you see them simply as entities to manipulate. Prepare yourself to comfortably defend the media and your organization to each other. One of the added benefits of this is when a question arises about media ethics or your industry's practices — you'll be ready to lend perspective, not just rattle off facts.

9. Be a Strategist

This is where proactive media relations comes in. Don't make the mistake of thinking that if you're not out there pumping up the organization's agenda every time you have a contact with a media person, you're not doing your job. Be selective in what you promote about your organization. Some surveys have found that 90 percent of all news releases end up in the garbage can.

Don't "over-PR" your organization, especially about personnel changes. Communicate the critically important changes, and target your media audiences carefully. Don't, for example, send your press release on the new Vice President of

Support Services to the local television news director. He couldn't care less, but the newspaper's business writer responsible for the "Promotions and Appointments" column will at least look at it.

Find the stories that could be of true interest to the news media, even if they won't directly showcase your organization. Determine the issues that affect your community, and suggest stories that are tied to those issues. Again, you will be remembered for your helpfulness and directness. Don't feel compelled to be a salesperson all the time.

10. Be a Team Player

This rule is really the internal version of Rule Number One. You'll find that becoming a team player is a great way to let your organization know how successfully you are practicing the preceding nine rules.

Seek out information from key people throughout your organization so you can stay apprised of critical developments. These may include, but certainly are not limited to: important shifts in company policies or strategic direction, noteworthy special events or projects, and acquisition of especially outstanding people or exceptional equipment. If you work for a large organization, staying current on significant developments is not as easy as it appears.

Keep others in your department who don't work in media relations apprised of your activities. The employee publication editor may find enormous value in the interview you arranged for Channel 10, and the government relations manager may need your help in identifying media perceptions of pending legislation that is controversial.

What does all this lead to? Building relationships and credibility both inside and outside your organization. In media relations, being a "good salesperson" with great ideas and dazzling approaches doesn't mean a thing if you don't build solid relationships. Your first task always is to convince people to care about what you have to say.

NewsSpeak Quiz

Media relations specialists need to familiarize themselves with the jargon of the news business. Below are 21 terms common to newsrooms. Match each term with the correct definition.

1. actuality
2. anchor interview
3. art
4. B roll/cover
5. breaking news
6. cop shop
7. hook
8. live shot
9. nat sound
10. newser/presser
11. package
12. pagination
13. phoner
14. reader
15. Sony sandwich
16. soundbite/SOT
17. talking head
18. VOSOT
19. voicer
20. wrap
21. tear sheets

SoundBites

A. an interview conducted by telephone.

B. police headquarters.

C. computerized newspaper page design.

D. a reporter's on-location live introduction and close for a pre-recorded TV news story.

E. a radio (or TV) news report voiced by a reporter and containing the voice of a newsmaker.

F. photograph(s) or graphics accompanying a newspaper story.

G. a news conference.

H. the recorded words of someone who is part of a TV news story.

I. a pre-recorded television news story voiced by a reporter.

J. interview conducted by a TV news anchor with a newsmaker who is out of the studio.

K. close-up video of a newsmaker or news person speaking.

L. a television news story with no accompanying video.

Chapter Two

M. news that's happening right now.

N. any audio that's part of a TV story but is not the sound of someone speaking directly into the camera or microphone.

O. a pre-recorded radio news story voiced by a reporter.

P. an on-scene TV news story reported either as it's happening or shortly afterward.

Q. video accompanying a TV news story.

R. the recorded words of someone who is part of a radio news story.

S. a TV news story read by the anchor with accompanying video that leads into the recorded words of a newsmaker.

T. a reason for doing this particular story at this particular time.

U. copies of a story that appeared.

Answers:

1. R   2. J   3. F   4. Q   5. M   6. B
7. T   8. P   9. N   10. G   11. I   12. C   13. A
14. L   15. D   16. H   17. K   18. S   19. O
20. E   21. U

Chapter 3

Attracting Reporters to Your Story

News is news is news, as every good reporter knows. Almost as enigmatic as Gertrude Stein's famous line, "A rose is a rose is a rose," this media truism still clues us into something extremely important in working with reporters. Although he or she may not say it, a good reporter can tell you how it feels in the bones when a story is shaping up to hold the page or take its special niche in the evening newscast. Lest we be too generous to our reporter friends, we probably should remember the famous Irish writer James Joyce and his classic assertion, "Every jackass going the roads thinks he has ideas." And perhaps we should balance Joyce's statement with that famous line from Gerard Manley Hopkins' *Felix Randal*. Speaking of the robust blacksmith felled by illness, Hopkins as priest says, "Ah well, God rest him all roads ever he offended."

Swimming confidently in the sea of ideas around him, a good reporter shapes the stories we receive via newspapers, radio, television and online computer services. These stories communicate the values by which we live and carry on our day to day enterprises. Caught up and sometimes overwhelmed by the busy-ness of business,

Chapter Three

we must help reporters become the word smiths they aspire to be, and in working with them we need be aware of and honor their values in communication.

What is News?

In the heyday of my reporting, I once asked several friends who are respected reporters, "What is news?" From each I got a different answer, but an answer which made sense to me professionally. Their definitions, differing as they did, carried my thinking to three significant variables that determine what makes news:

Who is making the decision? In most newsrooms, reporters, editors, and producers meet each day to discuss — and often argue about — what they believe is newsworthy. Strange as it seems, their discussions end in what one might call instinctual agreement: every news outlet in the city often leads with or headlines the same story. In this instance, the "big" story of the day looms large enough that everyone agrees. It's not always that easy, though, to decide what's important enough to fill the rest of the newscast or newspaper.

Naturally, each maker of news decisions is influenced by his or her own personal experiences, biases, likes and dislikes. The most persuasive person — or the one with the most power — wins out. In your dealings with the media, you need to keep this idea in mind: many a reporter has been ordered to cover a story while complaining to colleagues, "This isn't news!"

What medium fits the story? Certain stories obviously "play" better on television than in the newspaper, and vice versa. A marginally important story that isn't visual will most likely be passed over by television. A complicated, fact-filled but non-visual story works better in print. Newspapers, as you know, have more space to list things such as upcoming events, executive promotions, deaths, anniversaries and engagements.

What else is happening? News people dread "slow news days" when they must dig and scratch for something significant to fill the newscast or newspaper. Mondays and weekends commonly fall into that category. On slow news days, a desperate producer or editor will use stories that otherwise might not be considered newsworthy. Feature stories look more appealing then. So do "in-the-can" stories, "fillers" or "evergreen" stories — news which doesn't get old, but that can be plugged in at almost any time.

On the other hand, when a major story breaks, features, fillers and evergreen stories are no longer "news." On the day of the explosion of the space shuttle Challenger, the 1989 San Francisco earthquake, or the Oklahoma City bombing, there was little time or space for anything but the big story and supporting side bars.

Chapter Three

News Hangs on "Hooks"

You are most successful in pitching a story to a station, newspaper, or wire service when you have a news "hook." What makes this particular story important at this time for this news outlet's audience? Here are hooks news people look for when considering a story for publication. The more of these a story has, the more likely it is to be aired or printed.

Significance or consequence. What is the meaning or impact of the news? Stories with long-range significance are more likely to be considered "news." So are stories with moral or social importance.

When the space shuttle Challenger exploded on liftoff the morning of January 28, 1986, the impact was overwhelming. We watched in horror as seven modern day explorers simply vanished in a trailing cloud of vapor. At that moment, America's innocent vision of space travel died too. We no longer viewed the rise of rockets as routine as elevators going up and down.

Challenger's explosion also had far-reaching consequences. The space program stalled. In the past, we as a nation wholeheartedly supported space exploration. Now we began weighing the economic and human costs.

And the Challenger tragedy gave us another reason to doubt the integrity of our government. The investigation of the explosion allowed us for the first time to see inside NASA, an agency we had admired and respected. Internal documents cited sloppy workmanship, employee complacency and unreliable equipment. Most damaging was the investigation's ultimate conclusion: NASA had caused the explosion by forcing the takeoff despite concerns raised by contractor Morton Thiokol about the safety of the launch in temperatures below 40 degrees.

Magnitude. How big is the event? How many people does it affect? How striking are the visuals? A traffic accident with one fatality may go unreported, while an accident with five deaths makes news. Even though many more people die in cars each year than in airplanes, when it comes to news value, the magnitude of a jet crash killing dozens of people at one time outweighs the daily loss of life on the nation's highways.

The bombing on April 19, 1995 of the Alfred P. Murrah Federal Building in Oklahoma City would have been reported extensively no matter what the extent of the blast. It fit the first criteria — a significant story with far-reaching consequences as we realized our vulnerability to our own home-grown terrorists. But the magnitude of the explosion in addition to the massive loss of life — 168 people, including many children — made this a story we will never forget.

The magnitude of the San Francisco earthquake on October 17, 1989 made it an international story. California experiences numerous earth tremors, most of which barely warrant a mention on the evening news. But this earthquake measured 6.9 on the Richter scale and was carried live on TV as it shook Candlestick Park during game three of the World Series. When the dust and smoke settled, we witnessed the destruction — 62 people dead, a section of freeway collapsed like a Tinker Toy, and 100 thousand buildings in and around San Francisco either damaged or destroyed.

Timeliness. News is perishable. Today's news is not news tomorrow. Is the information fresh? Is it of current interest or is the topic viewed as passé? Has it already been reported by another news outlet? Is there another angle to the story which hasn't been reported yet?

Because of the timeliness factor, for several days after a major airplane crash, news outlets will be more likely to report even the most minor incidents involving planes — a non-injury accident, an emergency landing, a blown tire, etc.

If you teach a course on wilderness survival, the best time to try to get media interest is the day a hiker is reported missing or just before camping season begins. If you want to get publicity on credit card fraud or warn people about getting into debt by overusing their credit cards, a press release at the start of Christmas shopping season would be most likely to get media attention. And reporters would be more likely to do a story on prison overcrowding the day an inmate escapes or in conjunction with a riot or murder inside the prison.

SoundBites

Proximity. News, someone once said, is whatever happens to or near a journalist. That's probably a bit of an exaggeration, but, the closer to home an event or issue is, the more likely it will get coverage. Always ask yourself, "Does the story have proximity to the news outlet's audience?"

People tend to be more interested in something if it happens across the street versus across the state or across the ocean. Stories which may not be important enough to air nationally or internationally may still get heavy local play because of proximity. An athlete competing in the Olympics will get more coverage in his or her hometown than in other cities' media outlets. The story of a governor indicted for fraud will get heavy play for days and weeks in his own state, while stations and newspapers outside the state will give the story minimal mention or none at all.

Relationship to audience. Is the message useful to the TV station's viewers, the radio station's listeners or the newspaper's readers? A good test question to ask yourself is, "Who will care about this?" Then continue with the follow-up question, "Are the people who care reached by this news outlet?"

Human Interest. Is there an inherent emotional response that will move the audience, or a universal truth with which people will identify? Human intrest is a powerful element of all types of news stories.

Chapter Three

The three major events mentioned earlier — the Challenger explosion, the San Francisco earthquake and the Oklahoma City bombing — all evoked extreme emotional responses.

The explosion of the space shuttle became more poignant because Challenger carried the first civilian in space, New Hampshire teacher Christa McAuliffe. Children in classrooms across the country watched her launch — and her death.

While pictures of destruction in San Francisco mesmerized us, we responded emotionally to the stories of ordinary citizens who responded extraordinarily — those living near the collapsed freeway who rushed to rescue trapped motorists, electricians and carpenters who voluntarily showed up at dawn to help shore up buildings, and residents who carried hoses through the streets to help fight fires.

In Oklahoma City, the children most moved us. Parents had dropped their youngsters off at the America's Kids day-care center inside the Murrah Federal Building, trusting they'd be safe. A few minutes after 9 a.m., many of the children were dead. One terrible and tender image — printed in papers throughout the world — summed up the horror of the bombing: Firefighter Chris Fields cradling a dying child in his arms as he rushed her toward waiting emergency vehicles.

Conflict. Are there different forces pitted against one another? Often reporters try to create conflict or exaggerate it to make their stories more interesting. Political stories get extensive coverage because they almost always contain conflict. Victim stories appeal to reporters, especially if they can be classified as David vs Goliath — the little guy against government or big business or the "system." A group of residents complaining about the city, the apartment managment where they live, or a proposed factory in their area will almost always get coverage because the story has conflict.

Progress. Something indicating even a small gain for the human race can qualify as news. This could be everything from a proposed bill in the legislature, to a more effective way of teaching school children, to a possible cure for cancer.

Fame. Does the story involve someone or something of prominence? Well-known people, visiting dignitaries and experts can give an otherwise non-newsworthy story a "hook."

Of course, the O.J. Simpson trial wouldn't have been nearly as interesting to the American public if the main character hadn't been a star athlete and celebrity. The 1996 plane crash and death of Commerce Secretary Ron Brown in Bosnia received extensive coverage because of Brown's fame as well as the prominence of the other business leaders on board who perished.

Recently in my hometown, Phoenix, a car accident led every 6 p.m. newscast. Under normal circumstances, the accident wouldn't have been serious enough to be reported, let alone be

Chapter Three

the lead story. What made it important were the names of the injured passengers. Two children of former Phoenix Suns basketball star and now coach Danny Ainge were slightly hurt in the crash. Ainge's importance made the story important.

Unusualness. Is it a first-time occurrence? Is the story quirky, odd or rare? Are there any different angles that could catch the audience's attention? This category is endless. As a reporter, these were my favorite stories to do. One I remember most fondly told about a tourist item invented by Ray Roberts, a real character. At night, he would go out with a black light in the desert and catch unsuspecting scorpions. He stored them in jars in his refrigerator. Then, in his small factory, workers encased the scorpions in see-through plastic molds. Roberts' soundbites were colorful and full of his quirky personality. In one I remember he said, "They may be junk, but people buy them." The things still sell like crazy to people visiting the Southwest.

I just read an article in the newspaper—on the front page no less, complete with picture—that I would have loved to cover. According to the story, a New Age rage for promoting health is "ear coning." Practitioners put flaming cones in people's ears, claiming the foot-long candle-shaped object vacuums the sinuses and auditory canals of everything that doesn't belong there. I can imagine the great video we could have gotten and how much fun I could have had writing the story. (Don't try this at home!)

SoundBites

Credibility. Is the source reliable? Will other sources corroborate details?

Reporters, who tend to be cynical and suspicious, must believe you're telling the truth before they pursue a story. That's why exaggeration and hype can backfire. If the facts don't live up to your claims, your credibility is shot. Unfortunately, the media may not always stress credibility as much as some news sources, viewers and readers would like. Often someone can make unsubstantiated claims to a reporter who runs the story without verifying the information. Usually it's because the reporter doesn't have the time or resources to do the necessary research. Instead, he or she will try to balance the story by finding someone on the other side of the issue who will denounce the other person's claim. This works fine when there is no absolute "truth," just varying opinions. However, it doesn't serve the public well when there is an absolute truth that the media fails to get at the heart of.

News Categories

Journalists instinctively classify news into two categories: "hard" news and "soft" news. Generally, hard news speaks to the mind. Soft news speaks to the heart. Of course, not all stories fit neatly into one category or the other, and people will classify stories differently according to their particular perspective.

Most TV and radio stations, newspapers

and wire services actively seek out what they consider hard news. These stories are timely and important, and often have long term significance for the audience. And yes, many hard news stories appear "negative" to the public, leading to the assertion that the media is reporting only bad news. Even if people don't *want* to hear about these "hard" stories, many times the media believe they are fulfilling their public obligation by relating them. Hard news typically includes government decisions and actions, medical breakthroughs, natural disasters, crises, crimes, layoffs, economic statistics, and the creation of new jobs.

Soft news is news which touches us as human beings and works its way with our emotions. Usually it is much easier to come by, and many stations and publications employ it to fight the accusation of being negative. Often these are feature stories which aren't particularly timely or of lasting significance to the audience, but they are moving or offbeat. Sometimes called "fluff" stories because of their lack of substance, they still constitute an important portion of the menu media offer us.

If you intend to pitch story ideas to the media — whether hard or soft — consider carefully the leverage to be gained from these categories:

Local Angle. The local angle can exert great leverage. Newspapers, TV and radio stations go out of their way to bring every story as close to home as possible by giving local implications to national and international news. For example, when outfielder Cal Ripken broke the record for playing in the most consecutive baseball games, TV stations and newspapers all over the country localized the story by finding an employee in their city who had worked for his company without missing a day even longer than Ripken had performed for the Cubs.

Another example, this one of localizing a hard news story, came after the Oklahoma City bombing in 1995. In cities with Federal Buildings, many media did stories examining how their local structures were vulnerable to similar acts of terrorism. Other ways of localizing the story included talking to rescue workers and hospitals about how ready they would have been to handle a disaster of that magnitude in their city. Some news outlets investigated the existence of militia groups and the accessibility of bomb-making materials in their areas.

If you follow national and world events, you can often find a way to help the media enhance a story by using your organization to create a local angle.

Sidebars. This term became familiar to the public because of its use during the O.J. Simpson trial to designate confidential lawyer-judge conferences. It had long been used in the media to identify news stories generated in relation to a main story. When Pope John Paul II came to Phoenix, Arizona, while I was an anchor, we did numerous sidebar stories about preparations for the big event — the security precautions, sprucing up the city, getting the stadium ready, deciding where the Pope would stay, and choosing who would cook for him.

Similar sidebar stories aired regularly for months after Super Bowl XXX was awarded to Phoenix and the city made preparations. How would traffic flow? What would the economic impact be? How could local businesses make money from the event? Who would get tickets? What were landscaping experts doing to get the playing field in tip top shape?

If you react quickly after a story develops, you can sometimes entice the media to use your business or organization to expand the central story with a sidebar. Playing sidebar piggyback can be more than a game, even a rewarding business practice.

Hot Issues of the Day. Some hot issues of our day are the environment, crime, the Internet, and technology. Do you have a story you can relate to an issue on everyone's mind right now? If so, the media will be more likely to use it.

Trends and Innovations. The media regularly report on new trends or developments. Sometimes they aren't really "new," just repackaged a bit. Do you have a different way of doing things or an idea for improving something? Can you "create" a trend or help illustrate one already identified? If so, your chances of getting good coverage for your organization improve.

Interesting People/Places/Things.
These stories can be about anything, any place, or anyone who is unusual, visual or exciting: bungy jumping, a woman who raises llamas in the city, or rafting through the Grand Canyon. Charles Kuralt's "On the Road" stories fitted into this category and became a national treasure. Creative thought applied to the unique specifics of your organization can yield similar media attention.

Kids and/or Animals. It's true. Reporters
— and their audiences — can't resist stories about kids and/or animals. Jim Henson made a phenomenally successful business of turning the traits of kids and animals into the Muppets. A movie about a talking pig, *Babe*, not only found success at the box office, but also garnered a nomination for an Academy Award in 1996. The late E.B. White, distinguished author and humorist, humanized the mouse Stewart Little and gave him international citizenship. The late actor W.C. Fields reversed the process by exacting the humor from rejecting children: "Anyone who hates children can't be all bad."

Special Events. Awards, conferences, meet-
ings, contests, and groundbreakings can gener-

ate positive media exposure. Though not all will appeal to a reporter or photographer, you're most likely to get coverage in these circumstances: if the event is out of the ordinary, if you have an unusual theme, if the event is for an especially good cause, or if you have an unusual guest.

Also, don't underestimate the value of serving food at your event, especially close to lunch or dinner time. Reporters are often too busy to eat and can hardly resist the appeal of being able to get a meal (a free one, at that!) while they're working.

Help for the Audience. Information that obviously will help the audience can bring you great publicity. A home security company informs people how to avoid break-ins; an association of investment counselors explains how to pick a reliable financial advisor; a boating company promotes safety on the water. All generate media coverage and good will — even free advertising — for the sponsoring organization.

Success/Failure/Turnaround. Great successes, horrible failures and amazing turnarounds — all will interest reporters. You usually don't want to publicize a failure, but if the media comes to you about one, you can make the best of the bad happening by accepting responsibility thoughtfully and humanely. With equal considered judgment and grace, you can capitalize on your successes or on how you turned things around. Classic turnaround stories include Johnson and

SoundBites

Johnson's recovery after the Tylenol poisonings and Chrysler's return to financial success under Lee Iaccoca's leadership.

Holidays. You need not be highly creative to use the excitement and good will of holidays to your advantage. New Years, Christmas and Thanksgiving each generate dozens of stories yearly. You can use these nationally celebrated holidays to gain media attention, but you can also be equally successful in working with the lesser known commemorative events. Check your calendar or Chase's Annual Events, which lists thousands of special events and holidays on which you could piggyback a positive story. The book not only lists all state and national holidays, but also includes presidential proclamations, public holidays of other nations, astronomical phenomena and historic anniversaries.

Spot News. Spot news to the media is an extremely important category. Every news station and newspaper constantly monitors the major police and fire radio channels. These spontaneous events — fires, shootings, accidents, explosions, earthquakes, storms — make up a significant part of most news coverage. Spot news is usually beyond your control and not of your making. Publicity generated by spot news can often turn negative if not handled quickly and openly by your organization. These are the crises you must anticipate and prepare for.

Chapter Three

Develop a Media List

What media should you target with your story ideas and news releases? To build a media list from scratch, check newspapers and magazines for reporters who write about your topics. Don't ignore small publications. Even though their circulation isn't as high as larger publications, they may be more likely to use certain stories. Watch TV newscasts and listen to radio stations to learn the names of reporters and anchors. To get additional names, call the media outlets and ask what people would be most appropriate to receive your information. You may also have access to media directories (available in libraries) which list TV and radio stations, newspapers, wire services and magazines, as well as personnel. Many of these reference books quickly become dated as people change jobs so you should always call to verify names and positions.

Who should be on your list?

● *Newspapers.* Begin with specific reporters who write on issues that impact your organization. Among others to consider are the city editor, the editorial page editor, the business editor, and the lifestyle or feature editor. To make routine announcements about upcoming events and job promotions, include the editors in charge of those special listings.

SoundBites

● *TV Stations.* Put both the daily and weekend assignment editors on your list. Include any reporters you are acquainted with or who have covered your organization in the past. In addition, depending on your story, target the public service director, talk show hosts, and specific show producers.

● *Radio Stations.* Include the news director on your list as well as any reporters who have an interest in your topic or those you are acquainted with. If appropriate, also list talk show hosts and their producers.

● *TV and Radio Networks.* List the bureau chief, if there is one in your area, and specific correspondents. Also include producers of news shows such as the *Today Show*, *Good Morning America*, and NPR's *All Things Considered.*

● *Wire Service.* Include the bureau chief or news editor. If there is a broadcast editor, include him or her for stories appropriate for radio or TV.

● *Magazines and Trade Journals.* List the editor and any writers you are acquainted with.

List important information. Update your media list every six months. Stations drop or add shows. Publications change formats. Personnel change jobs. Releases addressed to people who aren't there to receive them will get tossed.

Chapter Three

Your media list is your most treasured resource in media relations. Keep yours on computer or hard copy with the following information:
- Name
- Title
- Company
- Address
- Phone (including, when appropriate, office, home, mobile, pager)
- Fax
- E-mail address
- Deadline
- Special Notes (Do they like phone calls or only written information? Do they accept outside photos or videotape? Is faxing preferable? Do they like E-mail?)

Deadline Guidelines

Reporters are always fighting deadlines. News is a perishable product which gets old in a matter of hours. If a reporter contacts you, respond immediately. Your window of opportunity could close quickly. Ascertain the deadline for your particular story and be sensitive to it.

If you do the contacting, understand the medium and its various deadlines. Try not to call a reporter near a deadline unless you are reporting or amending a breaking story. Check with the stations and publications on your media list for their specific deadlines, but here are some general guidelines:

SoundBites

● **Magazines.** Deadlines vary according to frequency of the publication. Guidelines for submission are available from most and can be had by contacting the editorial staff.

● **Morning Newspapers.** Deadline for general news: 4 p.m. of the day before publication. Late-breaking news: 8 p.m. of the day prior to issue. Major late-breaking news: 11 p.m. prior to the issue.

● **Afternoon Newspapers.** Deadline for general news: the day before. Late-breaking news: up to 10 a.m. of the day of issue. Major late-breaking news: 11 a.m. of day of issue.

● **Sunday Edition.** Deadline for features: Wednesday before the issue. News: Noon Saturday.

● **Television.** Deadlines for television stations depend on the times of the newscasts. Usually, the morning is best for contacting them. And most stations prefer to know of a planned event a couple of days in advance. Of course, TV stations and networks broadcast breaking news almost immediately.

● **Radio.** Talk shows book guests days or weeks in advance, but may change plans quickly if there's a hot issue they want to address.

Chapter Three

Radio stations and networks put breaking news on the air immediately.

News Releases: Avoid the Circular File

News outlets receive hundreds of news releases by mail, FAX and E-mail each week. Unfortunately, some don't even get opened and many go unread. Here are some ways you can maximize the chances your news releases will not only get read, but used:

Make it news not advertising. Look at your "news" the way reporters will. How does it relate to their audience? Is it unique, new or unusual? What is this news story's hook?

Avoid any hint of advertising in your news releases. When the media publicize your product or service at no cost to you, they do so because they are practicing journalism, not advertising. Your release is almost certain to get trashed if you prepare it unaware of the difference.

Journalists "smell" advertising when your release talks directly to the reader so you should avoid the word "you" or "your" in the headline or text. Newswriting usually talks in third-person. Instead of saying, "You can have the service of Nordstroms at the price of Wal-Mart," write "Customers can have the service of Nordstroms at the price of Wal-Mart."

SoundBites

Target Your Release. Distribute your news releases judiciously. Choose the appropriate publications, stations, reporters, editors or producers for each news story. Use names to personalize the release wherever possible.

Organizations constantly deluge news outlets with releases that are unsuitable for that particular station or publication. When this practice becomes habitual, the news releases of that organization find their way to the garbage can without anyone even opening them.

Don't use hype. Avoid the over-enthusiastic tone of an infomercial. Don't exaggerate, editorialize, or use exclamation marks! Stay away from unsupported self praise. When possible, attribute accolades or predictions about your product or service to third parties not connected to your company. For example, "This product is the best of its kind to hit the market in the last 10 years" is an unsupported opinion. You can fix it by saying, "According to Stanford University professor Josh Logan, this product is the best of its kind to hit the market in the last 10 years." Or you could give support to the statement by citing specific benefits: "Because of its ease of use, low cost and reliability, this product is the best of its kind to hit the market in the last 10 years."

Stay focused. Even though you might be tempted to include in the release everything that makes your organization newsworthy, don't. Concentrate on one central point in each news release, using only the background which supports that point. Diffuse copy dilutes the impact of your primary message. If you have multiple messages to tell, issue a series of releases.

Be specific. A person who reads your release should be able to visualize your product or understand how your service works. Let someone unfamiliar with what you're trying to publicize read it. If they can describe the product or service, your news release is probably on target.

Include details that help the reader grasp your concept. Instead of saying, "The book contains important information for new parents to follow when they have children," write "Seabrook's book lists ten principles for raising well-adjusted children." The release could even describe and apply a couple of the principles.

Don't "disappear." Often, an organization will send out dozens of news releases which pique reporters' interest. But when reporters call the contact on the release for more information, they're told the person they need to talk to is in a day-long meeting or on vacation for the next two weeks.

Make sure that when you send a release with a contact name on it, that person will be available to reporters who want to follow up. You may also want to include a home number so the contact is available after hours as well.

News Release Format

When writing news releases, use your company or organization stationery, or blank 8½ x 11 inch paper with your company name, address, phone and FAX. Place contact name and phone numbers (day and evening when appropriate) at the upper right of the first page. Type "For Immediate Release" or "Hold Until (Date, Time)" at the upper left or riht of the first page. Say "Hold" only when the release is sent out before the date you want the information to be made public. This tactic is used only in important releases.

Try to keep your news release to one or two pages. Reporters won't have the time or attention span to read more. Give them something they can read quickly and easily. If you have information that fills more than two pages, except in unusual circumstances, break it down into separate documents.

Headline. Write a succinct, snappy headline that grabs attention. Use action verbs. Print the headline in bold letters.

Dateline. Begin the first paragraph with a dateline in parentheses that includes the point of origin and the date: for example, (Washington, DC, June 1, 1997.) As an alternative, you can place the date in the upper right below the contact name and phone number.

Chapter Three

Lead. The first paragraph should generally provide all the basic information of the story. Remember, make this lead as interesting as possible. It may be all the reporter or editor reads to decide whether your story is newsworthy.

Content. Paragraphs following the first should be written in the "inverse pyramid" style. Give details in descending order of importance, the same way a newspaper story is written. That way, if your news release is printed as is (which doesn't happen very often except in smaller publications), the editor can cut copy from the bottom of the story as needed to fit the space available. Also, you'll keep the reader's interest longer.

Use short sentences and colorful words. Avoid jargon. Spell out all names and agencies in the first reference, then if appropriate follow with the abbreviation or acronym in parenthesis.

Try to use at least one meaningful quote from someone in your organization. The words should add information or interest to the news release rather than restating what has already been said.

Double-space your text and leave at least one inch margins. Check your grammar, spelling and accuracy. Sloppy releases make a bad impression. They cast doubt on the validity of your story and the credibility of your organization.

SoundBites

Boilerplate Paragraph. In many cases, you will want to complete your release with a standard closing paragraph — or boilerplate paragraph — that briefly describes the purpose, services, or work of your company or organization. Even if this portion of the release isn't used as written, the information gives editors and reporters important background information. You can use the same paragraph in all releases you send.

Ending. Put the word "more" (small m) at the bottom of the page if the copy continues. Number the following page or pages. Put the word "End" or -30- or # # # at the end of release.

Now we'll look at an actual News Release following the traditional format.

News Release Example

For Immediate Release
Contact: Marilyn Jamison
(617) 555-6017

SSOFF Merger Creates Computer Services Giant

BOSTON - (Sep. 1, 1997) - Software Strategies for the Office (SSOFF) will complete a merger with Denver-based Randman-Shay Computer Consulting, Inc. on Nov. 1, 1997, to become the nation's third largest software design and computer services company.

— more —

Chapter Three

SSOFF, with annual revenues exceeding $1 billion, designs and installs a variety of customized software programs for large, mid-sized and small corporate offices. The company specializes in business software, and its product line includes word-processing, spreadsheet, desktop publishing, graphic presentation, financial data, time management, clerical assistance, special event-planning and foreign language packages available in both PC and Macintosh formats.

Randman-Shay, with annual revenues of $250 million, analyzes the functionality of computer systems in large, mid-sized and small corporations and makes recommendations for enhancements.

"As a merged organization, we can offer our clients the complete spectrum of computer services," said SSOFF chairman and CEO J. Carroll "Carr" Stemmons III. "I'm confident that this is a productive move for our customers and our shareholders."

"We're delighted to be merging with such an outstanding organization," said Franklin H. Meier, chairman of Randman-Shay. "Each of our companies brings important expertise to the table, and essentially we complete each other."

Stemmons founded SSOFF in 1982 to address the growing need for manageable computer systems in corporate offices.

Randman-Shay was founded in 1984 to service computer systems in major corporations and in 1989 expanded to computer consulting. SSOFF has 9,000 employees in 27 offices across the country.

Randman-Shay has 2,500 employees in 30 markets nationwide. Both companies have offices in

— more —

SoundBites

New York, Los Angeles, San Francisco, Chicago, Dallas, Seattle, Atlanta, Cleveland, Detroit, Miami and Minneapolis. Currently, SSOFF does not have a presence in Denver; Randman-Shay does not have an office in Boston.

"The merger will give each of us an immediate presence in the other's home city, along with more than two dozen other markets," Meier said. "That's very exciting."

For more information about the merger or to arrange interviews, contact Marilyn Jamison at (617) 555-6017.

#

Here are two versions of a more feature oriented news release.

Feature News Release Examples

Version One

For Immediate Release
Contact: Marilyn Jamison
(617) 555-6017

<u>**SSOFF employees donate themselves
to the community**</u>

BOSTON - (July 3, 1997) - Thousands of employees of Software Strategies for the Office (SSOFF) have begun giving their time and talent to
— more —

community organizations in 27 cities across the country as part of a corporate policy that encourages and provides incentives for volunteerism.

"We've had an informal policy concerning volunteerism since 1990," said SSOFF chairman and CEO J. Carroll "Carr" Stemmons III. "Of our 9,000 employees in 27 markets, there has always been a significant percentage — about 40 percent — that regularly volunteer in their communities. But now we have more than 93 percent of our employees donating their time at least once a week to needy causes."

The formal policy was adopted in April. It calls for giving an employee an additional $4.00 a week if the employee documents and verifies at least one hour each week of volunteer time. The time can be spent in charitable endeavors including soup kitchens, literacy programs, homeless shelters, schools for homeless children, Habitat for Humanity, food banks, social service agencies and church or synagogue sponsored food and clothing drives.

"We want employees to give their time, in addition to any money they may want to donate," Stemmons said. "They only get the additional money in their paychecks if they indicate that they have donated their services."

The corporate commitment to volunteerism costs SSOFF more than half a million dollars a year in incentive payouts alone, not counting administrative expenses. "To us, it's more than worth it," Stemmons said.

"We are encouraging every employee to be a good citizen. It is the least we can return to a nation

— more —

SoundBites

that has been good to this company."

In addition to the individual volunteer program, SSOFF holds a yearly HELP Patrol event, where for one entire weekend, the work force collectively donates time to charitable causes.

"It's our way of letting our communities know we care," Stemmons said. "And it reaps big rewards for our employees in terms of feeling good about themselves. There's no better way to feel like you're contributing than giving your time to others."

SSOFF designs and installs a variety of customized software programs for large, mid-sized and small offices.

For more information about SSOFF's commitment to volunteerism, contact Marilyn Jamison at (617) 555-6017.

# # #

Version Two

**For Immediate Release
Contact: Marilyn Jamison
(617) 555-6017**

SSOFF employees donate themselves
to the community

BOSTON - (July 3, 1997) - Terri McShanley, a manager with Software Strategies for the Office, gives the 2-year-old sitting in her lap an extra squeeze and kisses the toddler lightly on the top of her head. "You're such a sweet girl," she says softly.

— more —

Chapter Three

The little girl is not Terri's daughter. She is an abused child who has been placed temporarily in a shelter for children in crisis. Terri is a regular volunteer at the shelter. "I read to the kids, I sing to them, I play with them. They need kind attention desperately."

Terri's commitment is part of a corporate strategy developed by SSOFF to promote volunteerism. Thousands of other SSOFF employees have begun giving their time and talent to community organizations in 27 cities across the country.

"We've had an informal policy concerning volunteerism since 1990," said SSOFF chairman and CEO J. Carroll "Carr" Stemmons III. "And of our 9,000 employees in 27 markets, there has always been a significant percentage — about 40 percent — that regularly volunteer in their communities. But now we have more than 93 percent of our employees donating their time at least once a week to needy causes."

The formal policy was adopted in April. It calls for giving an employee an additional $2.50 per pay period if the employee documents and verifies at least one hour each week of volunteer time. The time can be spent in any of ten kinds of charitable endeavors — including soup kitchens, literacy programs, homeless shelters, schools for homeless children, Habitat for Humanity, food banks, social service agencies, domestic abuse shelters, child crisis shelters and church or synagogue sponsored food and clothing drives.

"We want employees to give their time, in addition to any money they may want to donate," Stemmons said. "They only get the additional money if they indicate that they have donated their services."

— more —

SoundBites

The corporate commitment to volunteerism costs SSOFF more than half a million dollars a year in incentive payouts alone, not counting administrative expenses. "To us, it's more than worth it," Stemmons said.

"We're encouraging every one of our employees to be a good citizen. It's the least we can give back to a nation that has been good to this company."

In addition to the individual volunteer program, SSOFF holds a yearly HELP Patrol event, where for one entire weekend, the work force collectively donates time to charitable causes.

"It's our way of letting our communities know we care," Stemmons said. "And it reaps big rewards for our employees in terms of feeling good about themselves. There's no better way to feel like you're contributing than giving your time to others in need."

Terri McShanley agrees completely. "I love coming to this shelter to help out," she said. "Making a difference in people's lives is incredibly rewarding."

SSOFF designs and installs a variety of customized software programs for large, mid-sized and small offices. The company specializes in business software, and its product line includes word-processing, spreadsheet, desktop publishing, graphic presentation, financial data, time management, clerical assistance, special event-planning and foreign language packages available in both PC and Macintosh formats.

To interview Terri or other SSOFF employees, or for more information about SSOFF's commitment to volunteerism, contact Marilyn Jamison at (617) 555-6017.

# # #

Chapter Three

Media Advisory

Consider using a Media Advisory to supplement your news release, or in place of it. This is an easily readable, one-page announcement giving information about an upcoming event. Like the news release, it must list the *who, what, when, where, why* and *how* of the event.

National Version

For Immediate Release
October 1, 1997
Contact: Marilyn Jamison
(617) 555-6017

MEDIA ADVISORY

SSOFF employees join the 'HELP Patrol'

Who: Employees of Software Strategies for the Office (SSOFF), aka the "HELP Patrol"

What: Will fan out in 27 cities across the nation to donate time and talent to charitable organizations When: Beginning at 11 a.m. Eastern time on Saturday, Oct. 18, 1997 and concluding at 5 p.m. Eastern time on Sunday, Oct. 19

Where: In the following markets:

- Atlanta
- Austin, Tex.

- Paterson, N.J.
- Phoenix

— more —

121

SoundBites

- Baltimore
- Boston
- Chicago
- Cleveland
- Dallas
- Detroit
- Fargo, N.D.
- Indianapolis
- Kansas City, Mo.
- Madison, Wis.
- Minneapolis
- New York (Queens)
- Pittsburgh
- Portland, Ore.
- St. Louis
- San Francisco
- Santa Monica, Calif.
- Seattle
- Sioux City, Iowa
- Tulsa
- Las Vegas, Nev.
- Miami
- Nashville

Why: To promote the concept of volunteerism. The HELP Patrol is part of a corporate strategy to encourage all 9,000 SSOFF employees to volunteer in their communities. During the HELP Patrol weekend, thousands of SSOFF employees will work in or with soup kitchens, literacy programs, homeless shelters, Habitat for Humanity, food banks, social service agencies, domestic abuse shelters and child crisis shelters. Contact Marilyn Jamison to find out where SSOFF employees will be in your community.

# # #

Localized Version

For Immediate Release
October 1, 1997

Contact: Valerie Rollins
(602) 555-1234

Chapter Three

MEDIA ADVISORY

SSOFF employees join the 'HELP Patrol'

Who: The 250 employees of Software Strategies for the Office (SSOFF) in Phoenix, aka the "HELP Patrol."

What: will collectively donate their time and talent to four charitable organizations

When: 8 a.m.-2 p.m. on Saturday, Oct. 18, 1997 and 8 a.m.-2 p.m. Sunday, Oct. 19, 1997

Where: at the following locations:

• St. Joseph Charity Dining Room, 1234 E. Spencer.

• Central Phoenix Homeless Shelter, 142 W. Boxman.

• Vacant, but soon-to-be-occupied home, 4 Baltimore.

• Mary Andray Memorial Playground, 64 Kyle Blvd.

Why: To promote the concept of volunteerism. The HELP Patrol is part of a corporate strategy to encourage all 9,000 SSOFF employees across the country to volunteer. During the HELP Patrol weekend, SSOFF employees will work in or with soup kitchens, literacy programs, homeless shelters, Habitat for Humanity, food banks, social service agencies, domestic abuse shelters and child crisis shelters.

# # #

Fact Sheet

A fact sheet is an excellent way to supplement a press release with digestible bits of present, past and future information about your organization. You can give a fact sheet to a reporter who talks to you in person or FAX one to reporters who interviewed you over the phone so they will have additional written information as they compose their stories. There are no hard and fast rules about how Fact Sheets should be formatted, but there are guidelines to follow.

Use company letterhead or make sure you list your organization's name, address, FAX and phone number. Feature the name and phone number of the contact person. Type the words "Fact Sheet" as a title for the page. Date the Fact Sheet so a reporter referring to it later can determine the currency of the information it contains.

A good Fact Sheet contains short paragraphs or bullet points that give interesting and important information about your company, event, or product which can supplement a news release or stand alone. Try to keep the Fact Sheet to one or two pages, maximum.

FACT SHEET EXAMPLE

**Facts About
Software Strategies for the Office and
Randman-Shay Computer Consulting, Inc.**

Chapter Three

Sept. 1, 1997
For Immediate Release
Contact: Marilyn Jamison
(617) 555-6017

• Software Strategies for the Office also is known by its acronym, SSOFF.

• SSOFF was founded in 1982 by J. Carroll "Carr" Stemmons III to address the growing need f o r manageable computer systems in corporate offices. Stemmons was just 29 when he started the company. Initially, the company had 75 employees in four cities—Boston, Chicago, Minneapolis and Detroit.

• SSOFF's revenues in 1996 totaled $1.1 billion.

• SSOFF has 9,000 employees in 27 cities across the country.

• Randman-Shay Computer Services, Inc. was founded in 1984 by Michael K. Randman and Donald W. Shay to service computer systems in corporations.

• Randman and Shay sold the company to Franklin H. Meier in 1988.

• Randman-Shay's revenues in 1996 totaled $250.7 million.

• Randman-Shay has 2,500 employees in 30 markets nationwide.

— more —

SoundBites

• In 1989, Randman-Shay expanded to computer consulting and changed its corporate name to Randman-Shay Computer Consulting, Inc.

• Merger talks between the two companies began informally in November 1995 and progressed to serious negotiations in March 1996. The merger has been accomplished in phases and will be complete on Nov. 1, 1997.

• The merged organization will retain the name Software Strategies for the Office.

• No layoffs are anticipated as a result of the merger.

# # #

Press Kit or
Media Kit Ingredients

A Press Kit, or Media Kit as it is sometimes called, is a package of news releases and other information related to an event or story. If recipients find it valuable enough to keep as a reference, it can work as a long term publicity tool. The Press Kit helps newspeople report your story thoroughly in breadth and depth.

You can use a custom designed folder printed with your organization's name on the front, or an inexpensive pocket folder. Looseleaf notebooks, spiral-bound booklets and even large envelopes are also acceptable, but try to make your package as visually appealing as possible.

Chapter Three

Don't overwhelm the reporters and editors with information. Include only what you think will be useful. Some contents — such as black and white photos — would be quite appropriate for print reporters but of no use for the electronic media.

Consider these specifics in preparing your Press Kit:

- News release or releases
- Fact sheet or sheets
- List of story ideas
- Calendar of upcoming events
- History of the organization
- Biographies of key officials or leaders
- Photos of key people, products, or events
- Important drawings, sketches or graphs
- Reproductions of previous articles
- Brochures
- Annual report
- Quote sheet, containing public comments and endorsements of your products, personnel or organization
- A software disk with everything on it

Using photos for Positive Impact

In newspapers and magazines, a still photo with action or emotion — interest grabbers — is often more valuable than a story in transmitting your message. Other times, photos act as a valuable supplement to the written word. They illustrate and clarify a news story, drawing readers into the copy.

You can sometimes talk a publication into supplying its photographer or you can send your own photographs to accompany a press release. Editors look for pictures with good technical quality, so unless you're an expert photographer, you're probably better off to hire a professional. If you take your own shots, be creative. Catch people in action and unposed. Avoid standard headshots. Also avoid "cliche" shots such as two people with an award shaking hands, the dead-pan plaque presentation, the routine ground-breaking shots, and the boring luncheon pictures.

Send black and white glossies unless color is specifically requested. It's best to submit 8 x 10 photos, but 5 x 7's are acceptable. List and identify the people from left to right as they appear in the picture and double check name spellings. Make sure you have the subjects' written okay to publish their picture. Type captions and tape them to the back of the photo, including contact name and phone number. Don't expect the photos to be returned.

Media Relations in Cyberspace

Someday, paper news releases may become obsolete. Forget the U.S. Mail, FAX and phone — all communications with the media may eventually be done online. While we're certainly not there yet, surveys show the media, like the rest of us, are in transition. Some reporters and editors cling to the old ways of doing business, but many are dramatically increasing their use of the Internet and online services to get information for their stories. Those of you trying to pitch stories to the media must become familiar with this revolutionary way of communicating or you will get left in the dust. Here are some ways to please the media online:

Ask first. Find out if the particular reporter or editor likes to get E-mail messages and releases. If so, ask if you may send occasional, well-targeted story ideas by E-mail. If not, ask how they'd prefer you to deliver your messages and releases.

Be concise. The subject header of your E-mail message must capture the attention of the news person before he or she hits "delete." Make it catchy and to the point. Throughout the message, continue to be brief. Have a longer file prepared in the event the reporter asks for more information,

Be selective. Many publicity seekers make the same mistake online that they made by mail or FAX: they deluge news outlets with releases and information inappropriate for the publication or station. You must be even more sensitive to this error in judgment in cyberspace because of the ease of communication. All news media become annoyed when they have to scroll through line after line of junk mail.

Avoid long "To" lists. Long headers with multiple E-mail addresses immediately signal to reporters that the news release has been mass mailed and probably isn't worth their time. Target your release with care. If using multiple addressing, set your E-mail header so it won't show the recipient who else is getting your message.

Pick up the bill. You'd never call a reporter or editor collect. By the same token, make sure whatever E-mail system you use doesn't charge the recipient for the message.

News releases on the WWW. If you have set up a home page on the World Wide Web, post all news releases there. (If you don't have a home page, you should consider establishing one to keep up with your competition.) Many reporters like to have all past press releases available when they cover an unfamiliar product or company. That way they quickly get background from the company's perspective rather than relying solely on other reporters' past articles.

Follow-Up

You may follow up your news release with a phone call to the reporter or editor. If you do so, keep your call quick and to the point — and don't call close to deadline. Some news people prefer not to receive phone calls at all, while others like talking directly to news sources. Some reporters and editors want a call before you send a release. Keep track of their preferences for future reference and also their attitude toward FAXing. Sometimes it's necessary to FAX a last minute notification. An assignment editor I know encourages people to practice "safe FAX:" call before you FAX to prepare the station or publication to expect its arrival.

Personal Meetings

When possible, and if media contacts are receptive, arrange to meet reporters and editors in person to drop off your news release or to discuss your programs. Keep the meeting short. Simply and briefly explain your organization and its goals. Ask questions to better understand the reporter's or editor's needs. Leave a Press Kit or literature about your organization or company and most important, precise directions as to how you can be reached. Make sure the new media contact is added to your media list. Follow up the meeting with a thank-you note.

Busy reporters who are covering several stories each day usually won't make the time to meet you for breakfast or lunch to discuss your story ideas unless they see you as an especially valuable, ongoing news source. Beat reporters or trade reporters who cover you and your industry regularly are most likely to agree to longer meetings. You can offer to pick up the tab, but be aware that many news organizations forbid their reporters from taking gifts from sources and potential story subjects.

Video News Release

Companies are trying more and more to appeal to television's need for visuals with video news releases (VNR's). VNR's are prepackaged news stories distributed to stations on tape or by satellite. Many stations receive stacks of these prepackaged tapes that they have never looked at, let alone broadcast. Others, especially small market stations, welcome VNR's as an easy and economical way to supplement their own news coverage.

The biggest benefit of producing a VNR is this: you control the message and footage. But before you spend the time and money to produce a VNR of professional quality, consider carefully if it is the best way to disseminate your information. Find out which of the stations you deal with will be likely to use it. If your VNR is aired, you can get coverage that you otherwise wouldn't. If not, you will have wasted a lot of resources.

Should you decide to produce a VNR, here are some guides to follow:

Use professional production values.

Television stations definitely won't use poorly produced tapes. Hire a professional to help you script, shoot and edit. Use broadcast quality tape, not home video.

Make it flexible.

Stations will be more likely to use your VNR if they can tailor it to their needs. Don't graph names and locations which can't be removed. Separate the narration audio track from the natural sound track so stations can add their own voice-over. Consider adding after the VNR what in TV jargon is called "B-roll." This is unedited raw video which stations can use to rework the story as they see fit — making it shorter, changing the order of the shots, emphasizing different information. Almost certainly they will supply their own reporter or narrator.

Avoid advertising or hype.

Just because you control the message doesn't mean you should resort to producing an advertisement instead of a news story. Study how news is rendered, and practice that objectivity which distinguishes professional newscasts from advertising's built-in bias.

Satellite Media Tour

Advances in technology now allow a spokesperson to stay home while "traveling" around the world — via satellite — doing interviews with dozens of TV stations in a matter of hours. As news programs become more prevalent and more feature oriented, satellite feeds give producers a wealth of easily obtainable material to fill their broadcasts. Stations simply sign up in advance to accept the feeds from satellite providers who charge a fee to organize the tour.

Movie studios regularly schedule satellite tours for the stars to promote their latest big screen release. Drug companies developing new products use satellite tours (often with celebrity spokespeople) to reach a maximum number of people in a minimum amount of time. Authors can readily publicize their books without actually traveling from city to city. You may want to schedule a satellite tour when you have a story and interviewee with national appeal. Companies in crisis can also use the concept to talk to viewers across the country almost simultaneously.

Satellite Media Tours can be expensive, but may be cheap in comparison to the costs for airfare, hotel, meals and other travel expenses resulting from a traditional publicity tour.

Public Service Announcement

Non-profit organizations — or for-profit companies promoting a worthy cause not related to advertising — can take advantage of the free air time for Public Service Announcements (PSA's) offered by TV and radio stations. These are 10 to 60 second messages — similar to commercials — promoting an issue or cause. They provide valuable visibility for your organization even though they may run late at night or early in the morning when audience levels are low.

Radio stations will accept PSA's as preproduced audiotapes or written copy that their own announcers can read. Television stations require visuals along with the script. Sometimes they will help you produce the message with their on-camera talent, photographers and editors, but often you will have to produce the PSA yourself. Stations receive many more PSA's than they can use. To increase the chances yours will be aired, follow these tips:

Research station guidelines. Find out each station's requirements for PSA's. Include that information in your media list and observe those guidelines carefully. Stations usually don't allow anything that smacks of commercialism, and each PSA should be shaped to the individual station's preferred audio or video format.

Stress quality. Because your PSA competes with commercial advertisements, it needs to meet professional standards. Poorly shot and edited video won't be used. The script must appeal to the ear; the words must match the pictures.

Target stations. Don't necessarily contact every radio and TV station in your area. Instead,

SoundBites

concentrate on those which reach the audience you're aiming for.

Focus. Don't confuse your PSA's audience by including multiple messages. Focus on one main theme such as "Do drugs, do time," "Smoking kills," or "Don't drive drunk."

Be flexible. Find out what PSA lengths your target stations prefer. Send them a variety of spots so they can fit in exactly the one needed. Normally this will entail producing 10, 15, 30, 45 and 60 second versions.

PSA Examples

:30 Radio PSA on Volunteerism

ANNOUNCER VO (w/ music under):

President Clinton has urged all Americans to volunteer their time and their talent to needy organizations. Everyone has something to share with others who are less fortunate.

STEMMONS VO (no music):

I'm Carr Stemmons, CEO of Software Strategies for the Office. I encourage everyone to volunteer in the community. Whether it's reading to a neglected child in a shelter, or serving meals to the homeless, YOU can make a difference in other people's lives. Volunteer. It's a gift your community cannot do without.

LIVE ANNOUNCER TAG:

To find out more about volunteering here in (fill in name) County, call the (specific name) Volunteer Bureau at (give phone number).

:30 TV PSA on Volunteerism

VIDEO	AUDIO
	(sound under)
30-ish woman reading to a child on her lap in nursery-like setting	ANNOUNCER: This woman volunteers at a local crisis nursery every week.
50-ish man serving mashed potatoes to unkempt young man.	ANNOUNCER: This man volunteers at a soup kitchen twice each week.
20-ish man or teenage girl shelving canned goods at a food bank.	(sound under) ANNOUNCER: And this young person helps out every week at a food bank.
Carr Stemmons (on camera)	STEMMONS: I'm Carr Stemmons, CEO of Software Strategies for the Office. I encou-

rage everyone to volunteer like these folks. Whether it's reading to a neglected child in a shelter, or serving meals to the homeless, YOU can make a dif ference. Volunteer. It's a gift your community cannot do without.

Other Media Needs

All reporters whether TV, radio or print have one overriding desire: to find a good story that is new, unusual or controversial. But to succeed in establishing the quality of communication you desire, you can sometimes trade on the special needs of different types of media.

Television News Needs.

Video/Action. Video, preferably with action, is television's first priority. Without visuals, TV, "the visual medium," doesn't have much of a story. Often, the more difficult a story is to visualize, the less likely television is to report it. On the other hand, the more visual a story, the longer time it will be allotted.

TV news departments like to shoot their own video as much as possible. You can help persuade them to cover your story by providing opportunities for them to shoot colorful action

Chapter Three

video. They will use home video if it's one-of-a-kind. A good example of one-of-a-kind home video was the tape of Rodney King's beating by LA police in March 1991, which was played on every news station in the country.

Stations will sometimes use video provided by a company or organization, especially if the visuals are difficult or impossible to obtain on their own. If stations use this company-supplied "B-roll," they add their own script or reporter. Make sure any video you plan to give them is professionally shot. Most stations prefer raw or unedited video so they can edit it for their purposes.

Time. Time is television's other significant priority. Time, of necessity, keeps all TV stories short and focused. Their treatment tends to be black and white because there's no time to develop the finer distinctions that we might name shades of gray. TV reporters usually don't demand detail. Because time is so limited, they boil down complicated issues and information. Knowing this crucial second priority, you do well to keep any information you send to television stations short and concise.

Soundbites. Because time rules the TV world, soundbites have become the coin of the realm. A TV reporter may tape a long interview with you but only use a very small part of it on the air. That soundbite is considered boring if kept on longer than 10 or 15 seconds. Television reporters want you to give them clear, concise, conversational, catchy and colorful statements they can easily edit into soundbites from which to build their stories.

Radio News Needs.

Soundbites/Actualities. Like TV reporters, radio reporters often use only short bits of your interview, which they call "actualities." Whether they tape you over the phone or in person, they edit your interview. Occasionally, radio reporters will use live or unedited interviews during a talk show or news show. In all interviews, the five C's give your answers life and power.

Time. Radio stories as a general rule are even shorter than those on television. Newscasts are shorter too, but are repeated more often throughout the day. Interviews on talk shows vary in length may last as long as an hour.

Background Sound/Natural Sound. Sound is essential ingredient in radio, and of all media, radio has made sound the door to imaginative reality. Because radio reporters use background sound to give listeners the sense of being on the scene, they may come to your location to record natural sound.

Print Needs.

Details. Print reporters thrive on a menu of selected details. Sometimes they will "nitpick" you, wanting exact dates, locations, spellings —

the fine details and specifics that make their stories accurate, readable and memorable. They will respect your command of the facts about your enterprise.

Quotes. Print reporters seek meaty, interesting quotes, often from a variety of sources. If they interview you they are most likely to quote you when you supply words that will stand the test of print: being read and pondered by an engaged reader. Sometimes you may be interviewed and not quoted either because there was not room in the story or the interview was done strictly for background information. Also, if you were boring or unfocused, the reporter may not quote you unless you are absolutely essential to the story.

Pictures. Pictures are becoming more and more important to newspapers and magazines, thanks to the influence of television and the newspaper *USA Today.* Publications often will accept pictures from outside sources for publication or will send their own photographers to an event.

Background. Because print reporters tend to develop stories in more detail than TV and radio, their stories must convey depth and perspective. How does this event relate to what happened before? You will get on well with print reporters if you're prepared to help them flesh out their story with information unique to your particular point of view.

Chapter 4

Preparing for Your Media Interview

By definition, reporters are those who gather news, but any reporter worthy of the name is closer to being judge than fieldhand. He or she takes pride in deciding what is newsworthy, and appraising every word and picture that makes it so. To do their job well, reporters expect to be in control. They choose what stories to cover, whom to interview, and what portion of the interview to quote. In short, reporters tell stories as they see them.

Most people reporters interview — CEO's, managers, politicians, leaders of every stripe — are also accustomed to being in control. They have achieved their positions of power and influence by masterful leadership. They have called the plays and asked others to execute them. The prospect of giving up that control by submitting themselves to a media interview can be daunting. Why let someone else decide how to portray you and what you do? Better to keep out of the bright lights and stay in command, right? Wrong! In the process, you lose a valuable opportunity.

It's true, reporters do have ultimate con-

Chapter Four

trol. You won't get the questions submitted in advance, and you won't be able to approve the story before it airs on the 10 p.m. news or appears in the morning paper. The finished report probably won't turn out the way you would have done it. After they talk to you, reporters write and edit their version of the facts. But *during* the interview, you can have as much control of what happens as the reporter. The key is being very clear about the outcome you want.

Some people, after they finish talking to a reporter, have this reaction: "Whew, thank goodness I survived!" Why would you want to simply *survive* a media interview? What is the point of submitting yourself to the process if all you do is get through it in one piece? Your goal should be to *succeed*, to advance your agenda. That takes preparation.

Many people are tempted to wing it when they talk to reporters. Either they don't know how to prepare or they believe they don't need to prepare. Most of us get to a certain point in our careers where we think preparation is for others and not for us. Or perhaps we're more challenged by taking chances . . . living on the edge. Preparation is boring. We get lazy.

When Laurence Olivier, one of the best actors of our time, was knighted by the Queen of England, a reporter asked him, "To what do you attribute your great success?"

"Two things," Olivier responded. "The confidence to perform and the humility to prepare."

SoundBites

Like Olivier, we have to be humble enough to prepare for a media interview every time we do one. We must never get complacent because "winging it" is the easy road to failure. Whether you have five minutes or five hours, you need to go through four steps of preparation: *Buy time, Know the territory, Determine what they'll ask you, and Plan your agenda.*

Buy Time

You're sitting at your desk engrossed in writing a report that's due at the end of the day. The phone rings. You absent mindedly pick it up, say "hello," and then are jolted out of your reverie when the person on the other end states, "Hello. This is Doreen Johnson from the *Daily Gazette*. I'd like to talk to you about a lawsuit we understand will be filed against your company." Now the alarm should go off — *anything* you say after that is on the record and can be used in the reporter's story. Why would you want to begin such an important undertaking while caught off guard, with your mind focused on another project?

The smart thing to do is buy yourself some time to prepare. Don't feel obligated to do an interview the minute a reporter calls. Tell him or her you're in the middle of something right now — as you are — but that you would very much like to be part of the story. Find out the deadline. Does the reporter need the story in an hour or a week? Agree to call back in time to honor the deadline. That's important. Remain polite and confident throughout the conversation. Remember, the reporter is judging your credibility and likability the moment you pick up the telephone.

There is one instance when you should not have to buy time. If you have sent out a press release, expecting and wanting reporters to follow up, you should be ready to do the interview when they call. You already have had time to do your preparation.

When the interview begins and ends.

Remember that even if you don't believe you are officially doing an interview, anything you say to a reporter at any time — even at a cocktail party — might be quoted. There is no bell that goes off — ding! — signaling when the interview begins and ends.

A client in one of my training sessions said a reporter once called to chat and casually asked how things were going during the woman's term on the local hospital's Board of Directors. The client talked for a while about some of the problems and concerns board members were facing. The next morning she was surprised to find herself quoted on the front page of the paper. She didn't know she was doing an interview, but she should have.

Also, if a print reporter is interviewing you in person then closes his notebook or if the TV reporter tells the photographer to turn off the camera, supposedly signaling that the interview is

SoundBites

"over," continue to be vigilant about what you say. Reporters can take mental notes, so anything you say after that may still be used in the story. Also, just because you *think* a camera and microphone are turned off doesn't mean they necessarily are. The interview has never really ended until the reporter — and camera crew — are gone.

Many people have learned the danger of open microphones the hard way. In 1984, President Ronald Reagan was preparing for his regular radio broadcast to the nation. During a voice check for the technician to adjust the audio level, the president made a joke, saying: "My fellow Americans, I'm pleased to tell you today that I've signed legislation that will outlaw Russia forever. We begin bombing in five minutes." Two networks covered the talk but decided not to report the remark. However, it was leaked to other reporters and ended up in print. The Soviet Union said the quote revealed Reagan's true attitude toward the Soviet Union and his hypocrisy about the peace process.

Handling an ambush. An ambush interview occurs when a TV crew walks up to you totally unexpectedly with the camera rolling and the reporter firing questions at you. This is "confrontational journalism" made popular by shows like *20-20* and *60 Minutes* and copied by local TV investigative reporters. If you think about it, there are few "true" ambush interviews. You've usually had some kind of warning that it might happen. Per-

Chapter Four

haps you have refused to talk to the media or
have failed to return their phone calls. So, a crew
waits for you in the parking lot or on the sidewalk
in front of your house. Maybe they knock at your
door or barge into your office with the camera
already running.

In other cases of supposed ambush, the
media might rush up to you for a comment as
you leave a trial or a community meeting, or as
you arrive at the scene of your burning building.
Again, I don't think this qualifies as an ambush.
You can usually anticipate what reporters will want
to talk to you about, so you should prepare for
the possibility ahead of time.

If, however, you are taken totally off guard
by an ambush, don't get angry, put your hand in
the camera, or run away from reporters. That
entertaining video will definitely end up on the
evening news. Instead, calmly try to buy yourself
some time. Be forthright and honest. Tell reporters you'd like to answer their questions, but you
need a few minutes to gather your thoughts. Or
agree to meet them later in your office for an interview. If you absolutely don't want to talk to them
or can't talk to them, calmly explain why.

Know the Territory

Now that you've bought yourself some
time, find out as much as you can about what
you're getting yourself into before you actually
agree to the interview. Before you hang up with

147

the reporter, tell her you want to know the particulars of the story so you can make sure you can help her. Find out your part in the story. What should you be prepared to discuss?

Of course, you must always get the reporter's name and organization. If there's any question in your mind that this person is really who she says she is, nicely ask for a phone number to confirm her identity. Keep an ongoing record of reporters you talk to, when you talk to them, and where they work. This helps you compile your media list which is necessary to sustain enduring news relationships.

Find out the medium — TV, radio or print — and format — feature, hard news, live, taped — of the finished story. If it is a feature story, the reporter will be looking for lighter, more colorful material. If it is a hard news story, the questions are likely to be more factual in nature. If you are to appear on television or radio, you generally will have less time to make your points than when interviewing with a print reporter. If the interview is live, you won't be edited.

If possible, find out who else the reporter is interviewing? Your competition, your opponent, your critics? This helps you to better understand where you fit into the story and what kinds of challenges, accusations, etc. you might have to answer.

Can you discover what conclusions the reporter has reached so far? You may not like what you hear ("We have good reason to believe

Chapter Four

you're cheating your customers."), but at least you know where you stand. On the other hand, if the reporter has just begun the research, ("I just got assigned the story and you're the first person I've called.") you know you have an excellent opportunity to influence the direction of the piece.

What can you find out about the reporter's background and style? If you have enough preparation time, talk to others who might know about the specific reporter you're dealing with. Is this a Mike Wallace clone or a kid just out of college? How much does the reporter know about your industry? If she covers it regularly, she'll probably understand more than a generalist who covers a lot of different topics.

When possible, read the publication or watch the show you are scheduled to be part of. If you are unfamiliar with the publication or show, try to get information about who the audience is. Do keep in mind that you aren't just talking to the reporter, you're talking to the reporter's audience.

Agree on a time and location for the interview. Try to make it comfortable and convenient for you and the reporter. You may want to put a limit on the time you will give the reporter. A half hour to an hour is long enough for most stories. Don't make the mistake of thinking the more time you spend with a reporter, the better and more in-depth the story will be. Actually, the longer you talk, the more the reporter will have to cut. The better approach is for you to decide ahead of time what information to leave in and what to leave out. If you tell everything to the reporter, knowing that he'll cut out most of it, you're giving up a lot of control.

Arrange to record the interview, if possible. Not only does the tape provide a record of everything that was said if there are any questions later, but it lets you review your performance as you work at building your interview skills. In some states, only one person in a phone interview needs to know the conversation is being taped. In other states, both parties must know. Check your specific laws to be sure. Even if you tell the reporter on the phone or in person that you're recording, he shouldn't mind. Never tell him or her you want to be sure you're quoted accurately. Just politely say you'd like to have a record of the conversation to review your performance and make sure you gave correct information.

Determine What They'll Ask You

Once you've gotten the information you need by buying time and knowing the territory, begin step three of your preparation: determine what the reporter will ask you. Say something like: "What I understand is, you want to talk to me about our earnings and why second quarter sales were so good. Is that right?" You've put the reporter on notice that that's what you'll be prepared to talk about. This doesn't mean he won't

Chapter Four

ask about other things, but you're justified in saying you don't have the information because the reporter didn't tell you he would want it.

After you hang up the phone, agreeing to an interview, put on your "reporter's hat" and brainstorm the questions you are likely to be asked. Often it's more effective to get help with your preparation. Ask your staff or colleagues to research and rehearse with you. What questions would they ask if they were the reporter? How do your answers sound to them? You won't think of every single question, but you can probably come up with most of them.

Prepare for hostile questions. What are the worst things you could be asked? Is there any inside information the reporter may have found out? Are there any "dead bodies" the reporter could dig up? Where are you vulnerable? What don't you want the reporter to ask? Be prepared with an answer to each of these questions, an answer that includes your positive messages, and you'll feel a lot less nervous.

Expect uninformed questions. Reporters don't know your topic as well as you do. They usually don't have time to do in-depth research. Because of this, they may ask uninformed, even stupid, questions. Don't be judgmental and don't let even the most asinine questions throw you. Be prepared to educate reporters without talking down to them.

SoundBites

Often reporters begin the interview with a generalized question such as, "Tell me about this issue," or "What's happening here," or "Why this gathering today?" Have a first answer ready that sums up your position and begins to guide the interview in the direction you want it to go. Even such a simplistic question as "How do you feel" deserves a thoughtful response because the reporter needs your actual words to personalize the story.

Always have these answers. Be prepared for specific questions about you and your company. What does your organization do? What do you do? How does your organization fit into the overall industry? What does your organization give back to the community? How does your organization advance minorities and women? If your company is one that has established positions on current social, political or economic issues, be sure you're prepared to address them.

"What is your worst nightmare?" Reporters sometimes ask this question, hoping to get an interesting response. Many an executive, caught off guard, would like to take back his or her answer! ("I worry that our hydrogen tank will explode, killing everyone within a one mile radius.") Have an honest answer prepared that won't get you in trouble. ("I don't have many bad dreams. I know we're doing a good job of keeping our employees and the people who live near our facility safe.")

Chapter Four

Don't expect questions in advance.
Often I'm asked if interviewees can ask the reporter for the questions before the actual interview. You can ask — nicely — but usually you won't be able to get them. For one thing, reporters don't like the idea of having to submit questions in advance. They feel it takes away from the spontaneity of the interview. Some news organizations even have policies forbidding their reporters to release questions ahead of time.

And frankly, many times reporters don't know what they're going to ask until they get into the interview. Your answers may well lead to new questions. If they do give you the questions before the interview, you must expect some that aren't on the list. In general, reporters should be willing to give you ahead of time guidance on the kinds of questions they'll be asking.

Identify Your Agenda

This is the most important step in your preparation — the key to your success. Whether you have five hours or five minutes to prepare, you must identify your agenda for the interview. What points do you want to get across no matter what? If you could write the story yourself, what would it say? Sometimes, when clients and I discuss their media experiences, I'll ask, "Did you have an agenda for that interview?" Often they'll reply, "No, because I didn't know what they were going to ask me." A well-planned agenda will enable you to succeed in the interview no matter what they ask you.

Reporters usually approach you with some idea of their agenda. Sometimes, clients complain, they seem to have the story already written before they even talk to you. There are good reasons for this. They could have a very tight deadline, and in order to get the story done in time, they formulate it as they go along. Perhaps they've already talked to your opposition and are leaning in that direction by the time they get to you. Or maybe the editor has strongly suggested an angle that the reporter is trying to fit the story into. Reporters could also have personal opinions and feelings about your company or issue which slant them in a certain direction. (Even though reporters try to be fair and unbiased, they are human beings who sometimes find it difficult to deny their own emotions.) Other times, the reporter's agenda is simply one of wanting to be informed about the topic.

Whatever the reporter's agenda, you must approach the interview with a clear idea of what you want to accomplish. Go into the encounter with your agenda tattooed on your tongue! Otherwise, the reporter will have complete control, and you'll end up simply answering questions. Your objectives for the interview will be completely bypassed. After it's over, you'll sound like a number of the people I interviewed as a reporter, "But wait, you didn't ask me about . . ." Too late. You had your opportunity. The interview is over.

Chapter Four

Formulate key messages. Taking into account the subject of the interview, determine what you want to say. What three to five key positive messages do you want to get across in the interview no matter what? Even when doing an interview about a very positive topic with no apparent downside to it, you still must focus ahead of time on the messages you want to get across. I've seen many spokespersons ramble aimlessly, unable to give strong, clear answers when they should have been hitting the ball out of the park. It's usually because they didn't formulate their key messages ahead of time. They didn't think they had to.

Smart spokespersons never agree to an interview to just answer questions. They use it as an opportunity to answer questions in a way that gets their positive messages on the record. Many of us try so hard to give reporters what they want that we end up on that slippery slope of simply answering what they ask. They take us, whether we like it or not, down their path.

To succeed in a media interview, approach it on the offensive with *your* agenda. To react defensively to the reporter's agenda, is to lose the game. Here's an analogy. You're playing tennis with a friend. When she hits the ball to you, you simply stand there with your racket out and let the ball bounce off. You take no control over where it will go. That is the defensive way to play tennis. If you play offensively, you wait for the ball, then swing to hit it back, aiming it exactly where you want it to go in your opponent's court.

SoundBites

Successful interviewees plan their messages and continually hit them back to the reporter.

It's best to get your messages into the interview as quickly as possible and as often as possible. Plan colorful stories, supported by facts and statistics. Don't be afraid to repeat yourself. We normally avoid repetition because we're afraid of boring people. But during an interview, you must repeat your key messages — not necessarily in exact phrasing, but conveying the same ideas. You want reporters to keep running into your agenda everywhere they go in their notes or videotape.

What do I mean when I say formulate key positive messages for your agenda? Sometimes it's difficult to think positively because we're so focused on the problems we face every day. Let's use our nursing home example once more. You're doing an interview with the local TV station. You know reporters usually approach stories about your industry negatively and will probably ask some unkind questions. You can be aware of that possibility, but still be thinking of your positive agenda — the three or four messages you want to continually repeat — *with supporting evidence* — throughout the interview. For example:

1. Nursing homes provide an important service for patients when they most need help.

2. Nursing homes are staffed by caring, dedicated people.

3. Our first goal is rehabilitation; many patients are able to go home to productive lives.

Make the messages proactive, concise

and easy to understand. Show us how the glass is half full, countering those who say it's half empty. If you don't, no one else will.

Here's another example of what I mean by proactive messages. Let's say your company is trying to build a landfill on the east side of town. People who live nearby oppose the undertaking. You are asked to do an interview on the proposal. The reporter will also be talking to someone from the opposition. Some of your possible messages, identified ahead of time, might be:

1. We are committed to protecting the environment. We live here, too, and want to make the earth, air and water are safe for our children.

2. We will construct the safest landfill possible, using the best, most modern technology.

3. Our company has a long track record of successful waste management. We'll build on that record and will be constantly monitoring the landfill to head off potential problems.

Of course, "positive" messages are relative. If there's been a terrible tragedy at your facility, it's difficult to think of anything positive to say. In that case, you need to talk about what you did to prevent the tragedy, what you are going to do to investigate it fully, and what you will do to make sure it never happens again.

A special planning tip: If you find yourself doing a lot of phone interviews on the same topics, you can write your messages in your Rolodex, filed under the topic name. Then during your preparation, you can easily review them and even keep them in front of you as you do the interview.

SoundBites

Gear your agenda to the audience. Keep your audience in mind as you prepare these key messages. Every person tunes in regularly to radio station WII-FM: What's In It For Me? The answer you give to some questions will depend on whom you're trying to reach. Keep this in mind: reporters are not your audience. They're the conduit to your audience. Are you really talking to your employees? The business community? Consumers? Your positive messages should include benefits that relate to your target audience.

Here's an example: let's say you've developed a new product, a more efficient telephone system, soon to be marketed. You're doing an interview for the newspaper's business section. One of your positive messages might be: this new phone system will revolutionize business communications, making it cheaper and less time consuming to keep in touch with customers.

If you were doing an interview on the same topic for the employee newsletter or a trade publication, your message might change because that audience would be interested in different benefits: this new phone system will drastically increase our market share, providing additional income to keep our company healthy well into the 21st century.

Decide what you won't say. Set sensible limits for yourself before the interview. For example, if you are discussing an investigation or a personnel matter, you can only say so much about

Chapter Four

it publicly even though you may know a lot more. Decide how much you will say, and don't let the reporter push you to elaborate further.

Before you do any interview, be aware of any proprietary information you shouldn't reveal, such as company earnings, future expansion plans, product ingredients, etc.

Once you have a firm hold on the means of preparing for your media interview, you are free to devote yourself to that mastery which comes with practice. Unlike professional sports, where the crucial lessons are learned in preseason practice games, in business one must be prepared to play for keeps every time out. This is not to downplay the value of trial runs within your own organization. Or, the value of hiring a media expert to coach your staff. Whatever their nature, the practice sessions will enhance communication throughout your organization.

Use the following checklist to help in your preparation for an interview:

Preparation Checklist

Date of contact: _____

Time and location of interview _____
_____

Have you arranged to record it? _____

Reporter's name _____

SoundBites

Station or publication _____

Address _____

Phone_____ Fax_____

E-mail_____

Topic of the story_____
_____

Format of finished story (talk show, feature, etc.)
_____
_____

Reporter's technique (friendly, hostile, investigative, etc.)_____
_____

Reporter's experience with your industry_____
_____

Information needed from you_____
_____

Your part in the story_____

Who else is being interviewed?_____
_____

Who is your audience?_____
_____

Chapter Four

Other comments_____
_____
_____

Questions You'll Be Asked

Who_____

What _____

When_____

Where_____

Why _____

How_____
_____
_____

Hostile Questions_____
_____
_____
_____

Other Questions_____
_____
_____
_____

Key Messages_____
_____

SoundBites

_____
_____
_____
_____
_____

What you can't discuss about the topic_____
_____
_____
_____
_____

FOR OFFICE USE ONLY:

Routed to: _____

Response made:_____
_____

Clips filed:_____

Comments on reporter_____
_____

Follow-up needed:_____

Media kit sent:_____

Thank you sent: _____

Chapter 5

Use Proven Answering Techniques

Doing a media interview can be scary. A lot is on the line: your company's reputation and your credibility. If you've armed yourself with a positive agenda, you will feel more confident about taking advantage of the media opportunity.

Years ago, I was taught by a grizzled speech professor who said every good speaker had to feel confident, even uppity, about himself and his message. As I was mentally beginning to reject his sexist assertion — to label it the counsel of a crank — the speech teacher went on: "Feeling uppity about yourself, ladies, means you're in control of your subject; it means you'll feel free to stand up, speak up and shut up!" Whether you are male or female and whether yours is a stand-up or sit-down interview, I would urge you to remember my old teacher's advice.

Here are techniques that will enable you to answer questions from a position of strength so you can control the interview.

The Basics

Bridge to Your Message. This may be the most important answering technique in any interview. "Bridging" is simply a matter of taking the question you were asked and linking it to an answer you want to provide. Done correctly, a bridge takes you from the reporter's agenda to your agenda, without making it seem as if you're avoiding the question.

Remember, you are not doing an interview to simply answer questions. You are using it as an opportunity to state your agenda which you've identified during your preparation for the interview. To do that, those who are best at interviews have mastered the art of bridging. They acknowledge or answer the reporter's question, then shift to their own positive points and examples. In a sense, every question becomes an opportunity to "score" one of your messages. Ideally, everywhere a reporter goes in his notes, audiotape, or videotape, he'll run into one of your messages.

As we said in the last chapter, reporters usually approach a story with their own agenda in mind. It could be because they're doing a follow-up on something they've heard or read. They tend to believe the first viewpoint they've received until additional evidence convinces them otherwise. You have to be especially credible to change their opinions.

Reporters also may have a preconceived idea about a story because they're under extreme deadline pressure. They may have their story nearly written — at least in their head — because they have to turn it around so quickly. If you disagree with their preconceived idea, it makes their job more difficult. Like most people, they resist change. You must continue to stress your messages over and over. Bridging helps you do that.

Think of bridging as three steps. First: Quickly acknowledge the question. Second: Bridge. (A bridge is a transition phrase.) Third: State one of your previously identified messages.

Possible Bridges:

"However . . . "
"The real issue is . . ."
"Or another way to look at it is . . ."
"You might also want to know . . ."
"Let me put that in perspective . . ."
"However, our research shows . . ."
"That's only one way to look at it . . ."
"There's something else to consider..."
"What many of our clients find . . .

Let's say you manage a nursing home and a reporter asks you, "Isn't it true that helpless, elderly people are being abused every day in nursing homes?" (Step one: Quickly acknowledge the question) "There are some unfortunate, isolated incidents." (Step two: Bridge) "But if you look closer you'll find" (Step three: Your agenda) "the majority of nursing home staff, including ours, are loving, dedicated professionals who care for patients like family." I'm not telling you to avoid questions completely, like many of our politicians do. Question: "Senator did you take illegal campaign contributions?" Answer: "We've done so many things to serve the people in this state, to make sure they have access to Washington." He obviously ignored the question. That answer angers reporters as well audiences. That's why it's desirable for you to acknowledge the question with a brief answer, if necessary, before going on to state your case.

"Senator, did you take illegal campaign contributions?" Answer. "Absolutely not. I'll be glad to talk to you more when the investigation is complete. Until then, it's important to focus on how important it is for the people in this state to have access to Washington."

Reporters may try to bring you back again and again to their agenda. You just continue to bridge back to yours. It's like verbal sparring. "There they go again," you say, and you adroitly bring them back over to your side. Other times, once you bring a reporter over to your agenda, the follow-up questions flow naturally on that side of the river and allow you to control the interview.

Stay Positive. Think back to an oft-cited statement of former president Richard Nixon, "I am not a crook." If Nixon had said "I am an honest person" that quote would not have been nearly as memorable or repeated as often by the media. "I am not a crook" has survived since 1973 because it was negative and because it contained an interesting, loaded word, "crook."

Often the reporter originates loaded words. Let's say I ask, "Why are you cheating the pub-

Chapter Five

lic?" You answer vehemently, "We aren't cheating the public!" Now, I have succeeded in putting into your mouth those inflammatory words. Even though you denied my statement, the negative language is still accentuated for the readers and viewers, so that in the morning paper a headline can appear saying "XYZ Corp Claims, 'We're Not Cheating the Public'." Or I can use your denial in your own words on that night's newscast.

Don't repeat the reporter's negative language — even to deny it. Because they're controversial and interesting, negative statements often end up with quotation marks around them although the words themselves originated with the reporter. Often, the negative questions or statements the reporter makes include negative buzzwords such as "dump," "rip-off," "smut," "gouge" — the list goes on. You give validity to them and drum them even deeper into the audience's consciousness when you repeat them. Instead, characterize the situation positively, the way you want it to be remembered. The reporter asks, "Why have you dumped pollutants?" You answer, "Our company has always acted in an environmentally responsible manner."

Believe me, you will *often* be tempted to utter negative language because it feels so natural to repeat the words the reporter has said. At some point, in fourth or fifth grade I think, the well-intentioned teacher taught us to always repeat the question in our answer. In a media interview, that's okay if the question is positive, but resist the temptation if the question is negative.

SoundBites

Reporters resort regularly to when-did-you-stop-beating-your-wife type questions. Many of my clients get upset about this approach, but we need to accept it and not get sucked into it. That's a reporter's nature. And we're not going to change it. Often, reporters ask negative questions because they're playing the Devil's advocate. They're feeding you what the other side has said, so you can counter those claims. To them it is a game of wits and they expect you to be able to hit back whatever they throw at you.

Those experienced at being interviewed anticipate and know how to handle reporter's negative, buzzword loaded questions. I was in Virginia doing a speech the day after an election. Then-Governor Wilder's son had just been elected to public office in Richmond. Did the reporter walk up and ask the governor, "Aren't you proud your son is now in politics, following in your footsteps?" Of course not! The reporter instead said, "Is this the beginning of a political dynasty in Virginia?" Without missing a beat (and probably saying to himself, "There they go again!"), Governor Wilder ignored the negative and the dynasty buzzword by answering, "This is the continuation of good, caring government for Virginia."

One caution: I don't mean for you to be positive to the point of being Pollyanna-like, unrealistically denying problems exist. If you take that approach, no one will believe you and your credibility will suffer. Let us look again at our earlier example when a reporter asks about abuses in nursing homes. You cannot deny abuses happen and remain credible. What you can say is, "Those are unfortunate, isolated incidents." Then move — bridge — into your planned message: "The majority of nursing homes, including ours, are staffed by caring, dedicated people who treat their patients like family."

Hold Your Ground. Reporters are paid to ask questions. Often they ask the same ones over and over again in different ways, hoping you'll finally give them a more interesting answer. They want to get a better quote or soundbite than a reporter at a competing publication or station. Let's say a TV reporter asks you about your company earnings, which you don't want to release. You answer, "The company is doing very well, but we don't release specific figures." The TV reporter gives up. That afternoon, a newspaper reporter calls and asks you the same question, but he asks four times. Finally you're so frustrated you blurt out, "Okay, we made $20 million — and that's twice as much as the competition!"

When both stories run, the TV reporter looks like he was beaten on the story. His stock goes down at the station. His boss calls him on the carpet because he didn't get that quote from you. That's why reporters keep asking . . . and why to win the game you must keep answering the same way. No matter how diligently different reporters try to back you into a corner, keep to your messages and treat all reporters equally. If they ask the same question, give them the same answer, though it's a good idea to use different wording so your answers don't sound "canned."

Let's say you've decided ahead of time that, for whatever reason, you can only say so much about a particular issue. Even if you tell reporters you can't talk about something, there's a good chance they'll still ask, even when it seems futile. Expect them to ask, probably more than once, and have your answer ready over and over again if necessary.

Here's an example of a phone interviewee holding his ground:

Reporter: "I'm calling to confirm that a well-known attorney in St. Louis is being considered for the U.S. Attorney General position. His name is John Winston."

Spokesperson: "I'm sorry, I can't discuss that. We have a policy of not discussing presidential appointments until the President has made a decision and announces it."

Reporter: "What do you mean? A number of sources have already told us it's true. We just need confirmation."

Spokesperson: "We don't discuss anyone who's being considered. I'm afraid you'll just have to wait for the President's announcement."

Reporter: "Well, can you confirm or deny that he's being considered?"

Spokesperson: "As I said, we don't discuss it."

Reporter: "We were told by several people that he was at the White House today."

Chapter Five

Spokesperson: "We don't discuss Presidential appointments until they are announced officially."

Reporter: "Look, this is really important. John Winston is well-known in our local political scene and he worked very hard last election to help the President carry our state."

Spokesperson: "I'm sorry. I just don't have anything more to say. The White House doesn't talk about these things before they're announced."

Reporter: "Can you confirm that Winston was at the White House today?"

Spokesperson: "The President's public schedule is available to the press every day. But, he also has other appointments that aren't on the public schedule. I'm sorry, but I've told you everything I can."

Reporter: "When will you be able to tell me more so I can do the story? My deadline is coming up."

Spokesperson: "As I've said several times, the White House has a policy of not discussing personnel matters or appointments or timetables until the announcement is made. Here's the number you can call to check each day at extension 5427."

Reporter: "What's your comment about a statement from Senator Ralston's office that Winston is being considered?"

Spokesperson: "We won't discuss anything like that. I've told you our policy and that's all I can say. Thanks for calling."

Here's another example:

Reporter: "Why did you fire Joyce Jones?"

Spokesperson: "I'm sorry. As you know, that's a confidential personnel matter and I just can't talk about that specific case. I can tell you that we have a very strong history of treating our employees fairly."

Reporter: "Was it because she broke company policy?"

Spokesperson: "As I said, I can't discuss personnel matters because they are confidential."

Continue to do that as long as the reporter keeps asking. Again, it's verbal sparring. Don't get angry. Just continue to give your answer.

Show Empathy and Concern. In general, your discussions with the media should always show that your first priority is the public good. When audiences are angry or upset, or when there has been a tragedy, it's essential that you show real empathy and concern in your answers. People don't care what you know until they know that you care.

Let's say you work for a company that wants to expand its plant. Environmentalists have raised health issues that a reporter wants to discuss with you. "We talked to a resident who lives next to your plant. She says her son has leukemia and she believes air emissions from your facility are responsible. How do you respond?" Answer (with empathy): "It's a tragedy any time a child is ill. I'm sorry for the family. However, there is no evidence that connects our facility with the boy's illness. We meet all emissions regulations and, in many cases go beyond compliance."

Here's another example. A company has applied for permits to begin mining a rich gold deposit near a trout stream in a rural tourist area. During a public meeting, a local citizen raises this question: "Why should we allow you to jeopardize our beautiful river and the fish by allowing you to mine so close by?" Answer: "I understand your concern. We also are aware of the sensitivity of this area. That's why we have done extensive studies on every aspect of the environmental impact and we know we can ensure the river will not be affected by our operation."

Invert the Triangle. Picture a regular triangle with the point on top and the wider base on the bottom. This is the way many of us talk, write and answer questions. We start at the top and gradually build our case, giving the background information and adding on supporting statements. Finally — ta da! — we get to the bottom line. But in this age of short attention spans, chances are that reporters' eyes will glaze over or they'll interrupt you before you reach your bottom line.

With the media especially, but also in other important communications, we're more successful when we invert the triangle. Start with your bottom line, giving the basic information first. Then, if the audience or reporters tune out half way through your answer, at least they've heard your bottom line. Inverting the triangle also gives listeners a road map for where you are going with your answer. It sets a framework for them so they can follow you more easily.

Question: "Why are you running for senate?"

Triangle answer:

I
have
a number
of reasons. I think
people today don't trust their
public officials. Washington is full of
insiders. We need more people who aren't
part of that good-old-boy network. I am a respected
businesswoman and I believe I can make a difference.

Inverted triangle answer:

I think I can make a difference. I'm a respected
business person. I'm not part of the good-
old-boy network that has closed
itself to the public good.
We need people in
Washington who
can earn back
the voters'
trust.

Notice the answer is more effective when you invert the triangle, starting with the bottom line, "I think I can make a difference. I'm a respected business person and not part of the good-old-boy network that's closed itself to the public good . . ."

Be Concise. Often when people are misquoted or taken out of context, it's partly their own fault. They talk around and around, on and on, never getting to the point. The reporter can't capture the essence of the message.

To be most effective and successful in getting your messages across, you must be concise. Boil down your information to the most important points. That way the reporter won't get lost in your words, or lose interest half way through your statement.

As noted previously, TV and radio reporters live by the soundbite. Let's briefly review what this means. Because of time limitations, individual stories are short, often just 30 seconds or a minute. Reporters may interview you for 10 or 15 minutes. After they chop up the interview, you appear on the newscast for 10 seconds! You're lucky to get one or two of those soundbites in a story. It's like a video bumper sticker. Similar to a written quote, it's a catchy concise statement, such as President Bill Clinton's comment on affirmative action, "Mend it, don't end it." While the average length of a soundbite these days is eight or nine seconds, many times a soundbite gets shortened to only three to four seconds. The media know we have short attention spans and to keep us from changing the channel, they keep things moving.

It sounds absurd. What can you say in so little time? Again, with practice, you can learn to say a plenty! It may not seem like much time to make your point, but if you plan ahead, prioritize your information, and *practice*, you can learn to say a lot in a little time. Try it!

Print reporters live by the quote. They want to use your opinions and ideas in your own words to give life to their stories. Usually a quote is just a sentence or two. During a phone interview, you'll probably hear reporters typing on their computers, trying to get your words down as you speak. In person, they'll be writing in their notebook. In either case, they may ask to record you on tape.

The following article, written by Bill Hart and used by permission, appeared in The Phoenix Gazette. He takes a wry look at being misquoted.

Reporters hear it all the time: "Sorry, I don't talk to the press anymore," the person asked for an interview says grimly. "Used to. Then I got burned. Never again."

Burned. That is: misquoted, misrepresented, misinterpreted all in that most public of places, a newspaper story.

What's wrong with us in this business? Why do we do it?

Three possibilities: 1) We are evil; 2) We are fallible; 3) It's partially your fault.

Hmmmm, I pick . . . number 3!

Chapter Five

Number 1? I'd be the last person to deny that evil exists in the world. Sure, some of us in the news biz are bad guys. In general, though, journalism doesn't pay well enough to attract your real villains.

Are we fallible? Extremely.

In our defense, I'd note that it's sometimes hard to understand what you're saying. Ever read the transcript of a court hearing? Even overpaid lawyers and silver-haired judges habitually sound brain-damaged swallowing words, mangling grammar, spewing forth bizarre thought fragments instead of sentences.

Still, it's true that we're supposed to know how to get it right. And that too often we don't.

But I'd respectfully direct your attention to Number 3. Many are the angry callers who begin by complaining of having been misquoted, only to concede after discussion that, yes, maybe they did say those words.

But that's not what I meant, they add fiercely.

It's a real problem. But what's a reporter to do — stop after each pithy statement and ask, "Do you really mean that?" That would ensure that almost nothing of substance, wit or true feeling would ever appear in our pages.

We think one of our duties is to pass on information that is as raw and unsanitized as possible. We must go by the words you utter.

Another point: Say a reporter is doing a story on a gun store. Say the owner divulges to the scribbling scribe that, frankly, he questions the stability of some of the people who come in to buy weapons and ammo.

Reporter writes story, includes quote.

SoundBites

Store owner is outraged. In fact, something similar just happened to a *Gazette* reporter. That angry store owner told us, "Your job is to make us look good!"

No. Our job is to report the key elements of what we see and hear; with as little regard as possible for whom it helps or hurts. Yes, we must use judgment. But here's a tip: Never make the mistake of believing that a reporter necessarily has your best interests in mind. That's an excellent way to get burned. Even if you didn't really mean it.

Bill Hart
The Phoenix Gazette

Keep Your Cool. You may have a perfect right to lose your temper with reporters. They can be rude, pushy and accusatory. They can ask loaded questions. But even though you have a right to get angry, if you do, you lose. We don't trust people who can't keep their cool in public. Credibility equals calm. We saw this the first time Mark Furman testified in the O.J. Simpson murder trial. After he endured lengthy cross examination by defense attorneys, the news stories that evening emphasized not what he said, but the importance of his demeanor: "Mark Furman kept his cool under heavy cross examination today." (Of course, we later found out that Furman had blatantly lied during his testimony about being a racist and using the "N" word.)

Also, the audience usually won't see what made you angry. Because the reporter's ques-

Chapter Five

tion won't appear, no one will know the reporter was hostile or rude or asked the same question five times. They'll just hear or read your snippy reply, and you'll lose credibility. You must stay calm even if the reporter isn't. Don't take his or her hostility personally. Answer by giving information, not denials.

Here's an example of what *not* to do. A sheriff, running for re-election, appeared at a community meeting to talk to citizens about issues facing his department. One of the audience members asked him a question that hit a hot button: a multiple murder case that the media and others had accused his officers of bungling. Instead of using the opportunity to explain his side of the story, the sheriff chose to get into an argument.

Sheriff (in a defensive tone of voice): "Perhaps you'd like to explain what we did wrong in your opinion." Citizen: "It's not my opinion. I'm asking you." Sheriff: "You're bringing it up. You need to tell me what we've done wrong." Citizen: "Well, apparently . . . " Sheriff: (folding his arms across his chest) "Don't use 'apparently' and 'seems' and 'uninformed sources.' Tell me what you think I did wrong." Citizen: "I only know what I read in the newspaper." That's all he still knows because the sheriff didn't do anything to enlighten him further. A television camera videotaped the meeting and this exchange appeared on the evening news. That public appearance was one of his last, the sheriff lost the election.

You *can* show righteous indignation to the media, but only if it is controlled. Calmly express

your resentment at having your honesty ques-
tioned, or tell the reporter you feel his questions
are loaded. The key words here are calm and
controlled as you say something like this, "I
wouldn't work for a company that doesn't care
about the environment. I live here, too. My kids
drink the water and breathe the air."

If, despite what you've just read, you want
to guarantee you'll make the evening news, get
aggressive and try to block a camera with your
hand. You've now challenged the photographer
who will keep the videotape rolling. It's like a
badge of courage. When the photographer goes
back to the station and tells the producer about
the encounter, you almost certainly will make the
evening news and may even be the lead story.
The topic of the story is secondary. You've made
it entertainment!

Avoid Jargon. Yours, like every business, has
its own special language and jargon. You're so
used to talking a specialist's jargon, you forget
that other people may not understand what you're
saying. When interviewing with reporters, you
must edit yourself carefully while keeping your
audience in mind. This also means avoiding acronyms whenever possible, unless you're sure
the audience will understand them or you can
explain them in your answer. Even if reporters
understand what you're saying, there's a good
chance they won't use a good quote or soundbite
that contains jargon. They'll have to spend too
much time explaining it to the audience.

Chapter Five

Pause. There's no reason you have to immediately blurt out your answer. Take a two or three second pause to think about how you want to frame your answer. This also helps you start with the bottom line and avoid repeating negatives. If you're doing a newspaper interview, the audience will never know whether you paused or not. If it's a taped TV or radio interview, the pause will probably be cut out. However, the pause must be silent while you continue to make eye contact with the interviewer. If you stammer and "um" and "ah," with your eyes shifting from side to side, the editor may leave the pause in and you will look like you're lying, trying to avoid the question, or hoping to dream up a whitewashed answer.

Even during a live TV interview, don't hesitate to pause if you need to, before you answer a question. To the audience, you'll come across as someone who carefully ponders an issue. Sometimes if you answer too quickly, you can sound "canned."

Keep in mind one kind of situation when such a pause may get you in trouble — if you are asked something that you must obviously answer "yes" or "no" to immediately. For example, a reporter asks, "Is your company doing a good job in the community?" If you pause too long, it will seem as if you have some hidden concerns or are answering "no." The best way to handle this is to quickly answer "yes," then pause if necessary to shape your follow-up thought, which will, with practice, become a quotable soundbite.

SoundBites

Tricks of the Trade

Admit Mistakes. What if Richard Nixon had admitted early on that he was involved in the Watergate cover-up and had apologized to the American people? Many political experts believe Nixon's presidency would have been saved. Instead, Nixon stonewalled. With impeachment impending, he became the first person to ever resign from the nation's highest office.

We are more likely to trust and forgive people who admit a mistake, apologize for it, and promise never to do it again. The reason Exxon continued to suffer after the Valdez oil spill is not what it did to Prince William Sound. It's what it did in failing to apologize. The public is still exacting a penance from Exxon.

Another oil company, British Petroleum, had a spill in Long Beach, California after Valdez, but came out with a positive public perception. A key event was the CEO's response to a TV reporter's question, "Is this spill your fault?" He answered, "Our lawyers tell us it's not our fault, but we feel like it's our fault and we're going to act like it's our fault." A brilliant answer which made the lawyers unhappy, but told the public the company took responsibility for the accident.

Hesitate to Speculate. Don't let a reporter get you to speculate on things that may get you into trouble. If you are asked, "When do you expect the cleanup to be finished?" If you give a

182

date and don't meet the deadline, the statement will haunt you. Instead say, "I can't speculate. I can tell you we will do it as quickly as possible."

Speculation can indeed be helpful in some cases, though. When it's to your benefit to speculate on an outcome, by all means do it. "What will happen if the Salvation Army doesn't get more donations." You reply, "We won't be able to help those who are most needy in our city."

Here's an example of a tougher question: "If your bid for the Senate fails and the Republicans control Congress, will you still be active in national politics?" Answering these kinds of questions is usually "no win." But again, you can use the reporter's question to your advantage: "I don't have a crystal ball, but I am totally committed to this campaign and plan to win on my record."

Flag What's Important. You can help the audience and the reporter key in on your messages by emphasizing or "flagging" what you consider most important. When you say things like "The main point to remember is. . ." or "The most important thing we've talked about is. . ." the reporters may even star this information so they know what to emphasize in the story. When you use this technique during a TV or radio interview, the reporter may be more inclined to include that particular soundbite in the story.

Correct False "Facts." Politely correct errors or wrong information in the reporter's question, then go on to finish your answer. If you don't correct the false facts, the reporter will assume you're confirming them.

Here's an example of what I mean. A reporter is interviewing a lieutenant from the State Police about traffic accidents. She says, "Last month alone we had 50 traffic deaths in the state. What is your department doing to reduce the numbers of serious accidents?"

The statistic of 50 deaths is incorrect. If the police lieutenant goes on to answer the question about reducing accidents without correcting the wrong number, he will in essence be confirming it. Instead he must answer this way. "That number is incorrect. We had five traffic deaths in the state last month. That's five too many and we're working to reduce that number even more by beefing up our patrols on the interstates and other major arteries."

Don't Let Reporters Put Words in Your Mouth.

Say what you want to say in your own words. Reporters like to simplify things into good/bad, right/wrong or success/failure. Don't let them get you to buy into their characterization by putting words in your mouth. Use the opportunity to repeat one of your positive messages.

Question: "So what you're saying is the program is a failure . . ."

Answer: "I'm saying that while some things have gone wrong, overall we're pleased with the results."

Chapter Five

Don't Be A Know-It-All. Let yourself say "I don't know" when appropriate. This seems difficult for many of my clients. Successful people often feel they are expected to know everything possible about a given topic, or that it's a sign of weakness to not have total command of all facts in their area of endeavor, so they try to answer a question with information they *think* is correct. Bad move. If the reporter finds out your facts are wrong, he may think you were lying and won't trust you again. Instead, tell the reporter you're not sure of the exact figures. Offer to find out and get back to him. Make sure you follow through.

Conversely, don't use "I don't know" as a cop-out for questions you don't want to answer. If you're asked, "Why don't you have more minorities in management in your company?" then "I don't know" isn't an appropriate answer. If you're asked, without knowing ahead of time, "How many minorities are in management positions in your company?" — and you don't know the numbers — you can say, "I'm not sure of the exact figures. I'll get those for you if you need them. I can tell you that minority recruitment is a top priority for our company."

Don't Fill Silences. This is something a reporter does either on purpose or accidentally that gets you to say more than you want to say. Example: on the phone with print reporters, you'll often hear silences after you answer a question as they hurriedly type in what you say on their

SoundBites

computer keyboard. We have been conditioned to feel that silence is uncomfortable, so we fill it in with conversation — and that's when we usually stick our foot in our mouth.

TV reporters can do the same thing. You answer the question and they pause inordinately long or leave the microphone in your face, hoping you'll say more. Don't let the silence trap you into revealing things you don't want to say. The reporter has an obligation to keep the interview going. Don't worry about pleasing him by continuing to talk. When you're done with your answer, stop. Period. (As I write that word, I hear my old speech teacher's soundbite: "Stand up, speak up, shut up.")

If You Can't Say Something Nice . . .
Sometimes it's tempting to bad-mouth another person or company, but it rarely pays off. Reporters like to pit people against each other because it generates controversy and good copy for several days. Company A says something derogatory about Company B. The reporters go to Company B for a response the next day. Company B answers by accusing Company A of not telling the truth. On the third day, reporters go back to Company A, which again questions the veracity of Company B. And the story goes on and on, none of it putting you in a good light.

Meanwhile, the real story, your positive message, gets lost in the winter storm of icy words. Unless you have carefully thought out the

186

Chapter Five

ramifications of a public attack or criticism, it's much better to deflect a question that asks you to condemn another person or organization.

Example: "Do you think your company is more responsible than your competitor because you've taken extra safety procedures and avoided accidents?" Answer: "I'm not familiar with our competitor's procedures. I do know that safety is our number one concern and we're proud of our record."

If, after careful consideration, you feel you must go on the attack, you're less likely to hurt yourself when you criticize ideas, not people.

Use the Reporter's Name. Many of my clients wonder if it's beneficial to use the reporter's name while doing a TV interview. During my years as a reporter and anchor, I would have said "please don't." Today, as a media trainer and consultant, I say "yes, when appropriate."

Using a reporter's name lets you feel and sound to the audience as if you're on an equal basis with the person asking you questions. It appears friendly and conversational, and can help relax you while you're doing the interview. As a TV reporter, I didn't like people to use my name during the interview for one reason. If we edited the interview into a VO/SOT — copy read by the anchor with accompanying video, leading into a soundbite of the interviewee — the reporter would not be part of the story. Yet, unless the editor was able to cut out the use of the name, it would be disconcerting to the audience. If that happened, we might not use the soundbite at all.

On this side of the microphone, I have a different perspective. I think the benefits of using the reporter's name during the interview usually outweigh the inconvenience of their having to cut it out. Certainly, during a live TV or radio interview which will not be edited you should feel free to use the interviewer's name. During an interview that will be edited for air, I encourage you, if you feel comfortable doing so, to occasionally use the interviewer's name.

"Anything you want to add?" Many times reporters will ask this question or something similar at the end of an interview. Always take advantage of this one last opportunity to repeat your key messages. Not only does that mean the last thing the reporter hears is your positive points, but also I often found this was the best soundbite interviewees gave me because they were thinking about summarizing everything important they had just talked about. They were able to say it quickly, clearly and concisely. Even if the reporter doesn't ask the question, you can volunteer the summary statement: "Before we finish, let me say again that..."

Chapter 6

Watch Your
Nonverbal Communication

Our concern for words in communication has been an honest one: how do we consistently harness facts to give our messages staying power? Perhaps we are aiming at the truth that the English critic and poet Samuel Taylor Coleridge voiced when he said, "A great man introduces you to facts. A small man introduces you to himself." Your words are important and permanent, forever recorded in a newspaper's morgue or a station's tape library.

Having celebrated the power of facts in working with the media, we must now turn to two personal aspects of communication: vocals and visuals. The vocals — how you sound when you say it — and the visuals — how you look when you say it — are crucial. They determine the impact of your message.

For proof of this truth, let's focus on one of the most significant defining moments in American electoral history: the Nixon/Kennedy presidential debates of 1960. Four debates were agreed to by each side. The first, on domestic policy, was produced by CBS in Chicago on September 26. Republican candidate Richard M. Nixon held every advantage over his younger and less experienced Democratic opponent, John F. Kennedy. Nixon had spent eight years as Vice

SoundBites

President during the successful two-term presidency of Dwight D. Eisenhower and appeared to have spent a lifetime preparing for just such an encounter.

When the actual debate started, a strange phenomenon occurred. Despite his knowledge and his executive aplomb, on camera Nixon appeared the lesser of the two candidates. Kennedy, tanned and well-rested, seemed confident and relaxed, as though blessed with the litheness of ancestral Irish dancers. Nixon, whose admirable Quaker background had been a sustaining force throughout his life, plainly showed the strain of campaigning under handicap of a recent knee injury. Tense and haggard, he slouched and struggled to appear presidential. Almost as though smitten from within, his jowly countenance gleamed dark and desperate as sweat streaked through the powder aides had applied to cover his five o'clock shadow.

Of the estimated 65 to 70 million viewers witnessing Kennedy side by side with Nixon, most thought Kennedy won. They plainly accepted the picture as more important, for neither of the candidates carried the day by verbal message. Those who listened to the debate on radio generally agreed that the debate was a draw. Neither candidate appeared to score a victory.

Chapter Six

Understanding the "3 V's"

As we have seen, communication is multi-faceted. The verbal aspect is the essence of your message. Your vocal presentation becomes the catalyst in bringing that essence into being. Your visual presentation, at its best, enhances your message and certifies it as a valid experience for the viewer. What is vocal and visual becomes, for want of a better term, style. We may not like to admit this, but style often does overwhelm substance. And people today really do judge books by their cover. They may judge you that way, too.

Communication expert Bert Decker uses the analogy of a rocket delivery system to describe the relationship among the three V's of communication— verbal, vocal, and visual. The verbal message is like the payload of the rocket — the thing we want to deliver into space. It's extremely important. But it will never reach its target or make an impact without the rocket thrusters propelling it. The rocket thrusters — vocal and visual — are your nonverbal communicators. Without fully powered nonverbals, your message will scarcely get off the ground.

All systems — verbal, vocal, visual — have to be in synch. When they are, the receptor of your message will utter "Yes!" the classic universal affirmation. When the systems aren't in synch, chaos and confusion, the antithesis of effective communication, occur. We've all been at a meet-

191

ing or in the audience at a speech when Wally the manager says, "I'm excited about this new project," but Wally has spoken in a monotone with a frown on his face. His verbal message has told us, "I'm excited," but the nonverbal message says, "I couldn't care less." Verbal and nonverbal messages must match. When they don't, we believe the powerful nonverbal ones.

Although not in total agreement about percentages, communication experts say at least 65 percent of effectiveness in communication depends on nonverbals. They speculate this is because we learn to communicate nonverbally long before we learn to communicate with words. This was probably true of evolving homo sapiens and seems eminently true of human beings today. In the womb, we respond to Mother's heartbeat. Once born, we react to her smile, her soothing voice, and her touch while she nurses us.

Visual Communication

On Television. TV has made the case for visual communication once reserved for the Chinese contention that a picture is worth a thousand words. Surely the vast audience beholding the first Nixon/Kennedy electoral debate of 1960 would certify this aphorism. Even those who by political persuasion or affection supported Richard Nixon were quick to concede that visually he came out second best. This concession gives all

Chapter Six

the more reason for being concerned with visual performance in communication at every level.

At KPNX-TV Channel 12, the NBC affiliate in Phoenix where I worked for 11 years, there's a room lined with videotape copies of every story that has appeared on the newscasts over the last 15 years. They provide a chronological history of the words, voices, and faces from hundreds of interviews — public officials, health practitioners, corporate executives, everyday folks. A number of them come off as insightful and exciting people you would want to know and could get to know by watching them on their tapes. Most of those on the Channel 12 tapes, however, come off as people who could bore you to death. I watched it happen almost every day. Normal, fun, interesting men and women turned into zombies the moment the lights and camera went on. Their faces became lifeless, their bodies stiffened, and their voices sounded like a chorus of crows.

An interviewee who fears facing the camera loses the very things most needed to succeed on television: energy, enthusiasm and animation. You can make the most profound statement of your life, but if you don't do it with feeling, no one will hear or care. You will be remembered only as a talking head, and not a very interesting one at that. You will have conveyed the impression that you were not particularly interested in what you were saying, and what you were saying is not worthy of being said. The most important thing in any interview is to relax and be yourself! You'll be most successful when you transmit three positive qualities. 1.) Openness — "I am happy to talk to you;" 2.) Concern — "I really care;" and 3.) Authority — "I know what I'm talking about."

Reporters and the public want to see a comfortable, confident, friendly spokesperson.

Here are guides for succeeding in on-camera visual communication:

Location. Choose the location of your interview with awareness of total visual impact. By thinking ahead, you can optimize the chances of your interview being held in the best possible setting. Avoid doing television interviews behind your desk. It puts a barrier between you and your audience, and may make you appear distant and removed. Should you be pitted in a David and Goliath type story, the visual of you behind your desk invites an unflattering contrast between you, the big time executive, and the little person, who is perceived as a victim.

Also avoid doing the interview in a location with a background that colors your story negatively. If yours is the Merry-Go-Round that breaks down, injuring three children, try not to let yourself be interviewed standing before the toppled horses. If there's a fire at your facility due to your negligence, try not to be interviewed standing in front of the burning building. Although you should never order the TV crew to shoot the

Chapter Six

interview in a certain location (such action may make them even more determined to have their way), you should be prepared to negotiate politely. With forethought, you can settle on several suitable locations for almost any interview.

One added note drawn from my personal experience in TV reporting: when a TV crew puts you in a location with a bright light or the sun shining directly in your eyes, again politely negotiate a change. Tell them you can't think clearly while squinting and ask if they can reposition you.

Face. In TV, face is character; and the eyes, if not windows to the soul, are revelations of your engagement with your audience. Your face should not merely greet us, but welcome us. You should come across as the honest, confident and believable person you are. By being warm and friendly, you will certify the quality of your words.

Your face should be lighted from within with animation and energy. Your smile should become a second to your words. But make sure the smile is authentic and appropriate for the situation.

When talking about serious issues, be careful not to frown — with vertical lines accentuating a furrowed brow — although that may be your impulse to lend weight to your words. Frowns generally are perceived as closed, defensive or downright mean.

Instead practice using what communication expert Arch Lustberg calls an "open face," with eyebrows up and horizontal wrinkles in your

SoundBites

forehead. You still appear serious, but at the same time sincere and friendly. This is much more effective on camera (and in person) than the closed-face frown.

Eye Contact. During an interview, eye contact is the electrical circuit completing communication. If the eyes certify what is said, they will take your words to their intended destination. Whether looking at the interviewer or the camera, keep your eye contact strong and confident. By doing so, you'll come across as believable and committed to what you are saying.

During most television interviews, a reporter will come to your location with the crew. When the reporter is in the room talking to you, look at him or her. The camera is simply observing your conversation. When the reporter is in another location talking to you through an earpiece (sometimes called an "anchor interview"), you'll be asked to look directly at the camera. This is typical on programs like *Nightline* and the *Today Show,* but is also used as a technique in local news broadcasts.

Many people, while answering questions, tend to look away to think. That's okay if you don't overdo it. When done continuously, looking to the side may make you appear shifty-eyed. Looking up may give you that "I'm lost — somebody help me," appearance. Looking down, which conveys the idea of thoughtfulness, is best, but it too may appear evasive if done continuously.

Chapter Six

If you are being interviewed in a television studio, ignore the cameras and look at the person conducting the interview. When you are one of several guests, look at the person speaking. Even though you aren't talking, the director may take a reaction shot of you listening.

If you wear glasses but are comfortable without wearing them, take them off. They may become a barrier between you and your audience. But if you need the glasses, don't worry about them. Do make sure your glasses don't have photosensitive lenses which get darker when the TV lights hit them. In an interview outside, never wear sunglasses. Viewers expect to see your eyes. When they can't, you may come across as duplicitous and conniving.

Head. Nodding on-camera is much worse than nodding off in church. Avoid nodding while a reporter is asking a question. It's an active listening technique that many of us use. But on camera, nodding will signal you're agreeing with a reporter when oftentimes you must be prepared to take exception to what is said.

I have found some interviewees — most of them women — tend to tilt their head to one side or the other while doing an interview. When done often, this undermines credibility. Keep your head straight (but not rigid) and confident.

Gestures. Gestures are exceedingly important in TV communication. They tell the audience you are fully engaged with your subject, and they ease your performance before the camera. Even if your gestures are not seen by the audience because of the way the shot is framed, in making them you will feel and look more relaxed. Your body won't seem as stiff or your face as frozen.

To help yourself use gestures naturally, let your arms hang comfortably at your sides. If you clasp your hands behind you or in front of you in the fig leaf position or, worse yet, jam them in your pockets, you will find yourself locked in awkwardness. Also avoid jerky or distracting gestures.

Posture. How you stand or sit during the interview informs the audience in subtle and distinctive ways. When standing, strike a comfortable balance on both feet. Any rocking back and forth conveys impatience and uncertainty. When sitting, leaning back in your chair even slightly can make you appear arrogant, uncaring or sloppy. To look fully engaged with your subject and comfortable in that engagement, sit slightly forward with erect posture, being mindful not to hunch your shoulders.

And choose the chair with care. Really soft easy chairs or sofas encourage you to sink back. A chair with a straight back is best, one that doesn't swivel lest you end up moving back and forth nervously during the interview. Crossed legs are acceptable on television but only if achieved gracefully.

If you have a strong preference for standing or sitting during an interview, make your preference known to your interviewer, but don't insist on having your own way in such a minor matter.

Clothing. The case for clothing on television is sensibly simple: wear what fits the story and will convey the impression you want to make. Remember that your image, the person you really are, is magnified on television by your clothing. You always want to come across as credible. Classic clothing with simple lines and plain patterns works well for most interviews. Usually for men that means wearing a tie and coat (gray or navy look good). Women should consider a conservative suit or dress and avoid extremely short skirts, plunging necklines or any outfit which reveals an abundance of bare skin.

In some situations, more casual clothing is appropriate. (For example, a logger on the job or an executive visiting the construction site of his new building.) In some settings, you may want to take off your jacket for a less formal look. Judge whether you keep your jacket on by the impression you will make. In a crisis, to convey the message that you are hard at work to solve the problem, it would be natural for you to have your jacket off and your sleeves rolled up. Whatever you wear, always look pressed, never sloppy.

Some viewers may remember a TV story of former vice president Dan Quayle serving Thanksgiving dinner to people in a homeless shelter in a western city. He was dressed in a suit and tie. Because he wore formal clothing in an informal situation, the video labeled itself as a contrived photo-op. Quayle would have been more in tune with his setting if he'd been dressed in an apron or had at least been coatless, with shirt sleeves rolled up.

Color on television demands special consideration. The camera doesn't like extremes. Checks, plaids, herringbones, and busy prints, though attractive, may "dance" on camera. (Called the "moire effect"). Avoid bright white or black as your main colors. (Physicians: often the TV crew will specifically request your white coat so you look more official.) It's okay to have a white shirt underneath a jacket, but a light blue shirt looks better. In fact, the best overall color on television is blue. Almost any bright color usually looks good on television.

Here are a few helpful nitpicking no-no's on clothing and accessories. For women, avoid big scarves, frilly collars or anything that will take attention away from your face. Don't wear clunky, noisy jewelry. It's distracting. You can wear simple jewelry as long as it doesn't rub against the microphone when you move. For men, don't wear short socks in the television studio that allow a distracting gap of bare leg to show should you cross your legs.

Grooming. You may think of television as exciting and glamorous. Most television reporters and hosts gave up that illusion long ago. It's just a job they take for granted. They forget that for you to be on camera may be unnatural and unnerving. So when you do a television interview, be pre-

Chapter Six

pared to fend for yourself. Tend to your own grooming. Don't expect the crew to tell you that your hair is disheveled or you have a piece of spinach stuck between your front teeth. Check yourself in a mirror before going on camera. Is your hair neat? Collar down? Tie straight?

A couple of stray notes about hair. Dark roots show up even darker on television. If you color your hair you may want to get it redone before your interview. To be at ease throughout the interview, use a hairstyle which keeps your hair back off your face.

Make-up. Women should be aware that television is picky. Even if you don't normally wear cosmetics you should do so on television. Usually, your every-day makeup with a little extra blush will show you at your best. Base make-up will even out your complexion, and lipstick and blush prevent you from washing out. Make sure you are well-powdered and have your compact available for last minute touch-ups. Don't overdo your eye makeup.

If the studio has a make-up department (usually available only at the networks, large local stations, and syndicated programs), let their experts work their magic on you, but don't expect too much. I learned that lesson in 1980 when I had a chance to go to New York to appear live on the *Today Show*. I had written and produced a long feature on the retirement community, Sun City, Arizona, for my local station. The network wanted to re-run the story and invited me to personally introduce it on the *Today Show* set. Nervous, hardly able to sleep the night before, I arrived early at the NBC studios and was taken into the make-up room. Gene Shallit, the show's movie critic, was already being primped and powdered. I sat down in the chair next to him. As the make-up woman approached, looking me over, I said, "Make me beautiful."

Before she could say anything, Shallit chimed in, "That's typical. They come to the big city and expect miracles!"

Men may find the demands of studio TV make-up embarrassing, but they shouldn't. In a studio interview, men may be offered make-up and they should use it. The anchormen do. It helps even out one's complexion under the bright lights. Using powder to reduce nose and forehead shine is perfectly acceptable. If it's late in the day or if you have an extra heavy beard, you should shave before you go on TV. The camera accentuates a five o'clock shadow.

At the risk of making too much of a shadowy circumstance, one might sum up TV visuals by referring once more to the first Nixon/Kennedy debate of 1960. Standing before 70-million Americans viewing them on television, the two men came off as distinctively different in leadership capabilities. How much of the difference was attributable to the searching eye of the TV camera as it focused on each man's face is difficult to say. But we do know that since the 1960 presidential campaign, TV coverage has become the major force in choosing a leader for our nation.

Chapter Six

In Person. Even though you won't be on camera when talking in person to a print journalist, your visual communication is still critical. The reporter sizes you up within moments of meeting you, and continues to assess your visual signals throughout the interview. Those judgments help shape the resulting story.

If you don't make eye contact, appearing shifty or unsure, the reporter may doubt the truth or conviction behind your statements. If you lean back in your big chair with your hands behind your head, the reporter may interpret your body language as arrogant or cavalier. If you sit stiffly without using gestures, the reporter may think you are anxious with something to hide. If you frown constantly, showing no warmth or animation, the reporter may dislike you. That dislike colors how he feels about your message, too.

Carefully monitor your body language in person as you would while in front of the camera. Maintain constant eye contact; sit forward; use gestures; smile appropriately; show energy and animation; dress for the occasion; be polite and friendly. Treat the reporter as a valued customer or client. Getting your message told fairly and accurately may be the most important sale you ever make.

Using Visual Aids. Any time you can enhance your story with visual aids that support your messages, you are more likely to get your story told with greater depth and understanding. Even print or radio reporters who won't actually use your visuals in their stories will be able to better understand your issue, product or problem when you can visualize it for them.

News conferences are especially "dry" and non visual. Consider setting up charts, graphs, diagrams, pictures or props which illustrate your story. To be successful, the visuals must be simple, clear, and colorful. Don't clutter them with unnecessary detail. When invited into the television studio for an interview, bring visuals which can add to your story. The producer may choose not to use them, but at least you've made them available. Charts and pictures should be at least 8 x 10 in size — preferably horizontal to fit the way television pictures are oriented — so the TV camera can shoot them.

When a TV crew comes to your location, think of everything possible you can offer them to help visualize your story. If you will soon be breaking ground on a new building, make available the architectural diagrams or three dimensional model. If you are talking about a new heart surgery technique, use pictures or a model to illustrate how it works.

Vocal Communication

Whatever your visual message, it needs to be enhanced and enlarged by your vocal powers at their best. The human voice has, through-

Chapter Six

out time, made us the complex and astounding creatures we are. Your vocal powers create the public self we know. To ask you to communicate that public self at its best in the daily doings of your making a living is to ask a great deal. But that is the challenge, and you can meet that challenge by practicing vocal communication. In coaching those who aspire to be effective communicators, I have found these guides useful:

Inflection. Use vocal variation to honor the content of the message you wish to convey. You need only stand within the range of sound on any school yard at recess to appreciate the range of communication and meaning conveyed by the human voice. Children at play can teach you the fineness of vocal communication. How subtle and complete their highs and lows and everything in between. With them as role models you immediately grasp how essential it is that you be as dynamic as you can be when you are the speaker. The more convincingly dynamic you are, the more likely a print reporter will believe you and a TV reporter will soundbite you.

How I wished I could carry on tape the range of school yard sounds I have heard! That tape would have jarred and corrected countless people I interviewed who, having once been school yard virtuosos, had in business life become boring one-note monotonists. The lesson here is this simple: in speaking on camera or off, use inflection as the energizer it can be.

SoundBites

Where tonal emphasis falls can alter greatly the meaning of what is said. Take this sign from the old English pub: *What do you think we feed you for nothing and give you a drink.* How disastrous it proved for the poor traveler who ordered and ate a large meal thinking it was for free. Confronted by bill-due at the end of the meal, he said he did not owe a penny. "The sign said, 'What do you think? We feed you for nothing and give you a drink!'"

"Oh, no," said the proprietor of the inn. "You misread the sign. It reads this way: 'What! Do you think we feed you for nothing and give you a drink?'"

Or take the sentence from the court of law, "I never said he stole money." Little wonder the person reading the transcript of the trial was confused since that sentence can be read to convey six separate and contradicting meanings depending on what word is most inflected.

Volume. Without proper volume, the finest sound becomes mere noise. Our superb machines for controlling sound enable us to render sound at its appropriate power for precise meaning. Since this is true, you need only talk with your natural volume on telephone or television. The person controlling the sound will ask for a sound check to set your level. If you talk too softly, he or she will ask you to speak up a bit. Sometimes, excited by our message, we tend to shout. Don't. Ssshhh!

Chapter Six

Pace. How fast should you speak? Studies have shown that people who talk very slowly are perceived as not being as intelligent or persuasive as people who speak more quickly. Speaking slowly can also put you at a disadvantage when the reporter chops your interview into a ten second soundbite. But talking too quickly can be a problem as well, especially if you don't pause between sentences. You may project nervousness. If you do pause, don't fill the silence with empty sounds like *um, er, ah,* or *you know* which bore your listener and undermine credibility.

Attitude. Whenever we speak, our attitude may bleed through into our voices. If we are feeling angry, or defensive or put upon, our voices, without conscious control, give away our true feelings. And because our natural impulse is to match the voice quality of the person interviewing us, we need to exercise special control if the reporter asking the questions is strident or hostile. Match the voice quality of the people around only if their voices are pleasant and will contribute to the efficacy of your message.

The Telephone Interview.

Telephone interviews leave the human voice naked and exposed. Because there is no visual communication, your vocal quality takes on even greater significance. If you speak in a monotone, you'll appear bored or unconcerned.

SoundBites

If you talk too fast without pausing, you will sound nervous or uncertain. If you speak too slowly, you'll bore your audience, and may come across as less persuasive or less intelligent than you are.

Print and radio reporters do many phone interviews. Even television media may get information from you over the telephone for use in their stories.

Many people prefer talking to reporters by phone. They find it less threatening. They can relax in the comfort of their own office or home. Their appearance doesn't matter. They can easily refer to notes in front of them while they talk. They can practice nonverbal communication which will relax them, permit them to speak with normal cogency, and help them to be interpreted the way they wish to be interpreted.

Despite those advantages, the phone interview also presents special challenges. Review the following "Don'ts" before your interview:

Don't Let Your Guard Down. After a while on the phone, you may forget you are talking to a reporter who can quote everything you say. Keep reminding yourself that everything that comes out of your mouth can end up on the air or in print. And if you're doing a live radio interview over the phone known as a "phoner," what you say is immediately broadcast to thousands, maybe millions, of listeners. Also, while on the phone don't allow yourself to be distracted by things in your immediate vicinity or by people around you.

Chapter Six

Don't Fill Silences. Print reporters will be typing on their computers while you talk, trying to get down everything you say. In the meantime, you may hear a lot of dead air. Don't let the silence tempt you into continuing to talk when you may end up saying more than you intended.

Don't Use a Speaker Phone. A speaker phone, marvelous invention that it is, has one significant disadvantage: it makes you come across as remote and distant, maybe even arrogant. If you want someone else to participate in or listen to your conversation, arrange for a conference call or have them pick up an extension phone.

Don't Lose Energy. Because telephone interviews may cause us to feel distracted or extremely relaxed, we need to conduct them with special care. As we lean back, slumped in our chair, our voice loses its energy and animation. While the reporter asks about layoffs or plant accidents, we may sound unconcerned even though we really aren't. The reporter's perception may be reflected in the printed story: "When asked about the plant accident, spokesman J. Doe seemed unconcerned about the people injured." Truth was spokesman J. Doe was extremely concerned but the interview took place on a Friday night and he was exhausted from a hectic week.

SoundBites

Don't Sit. If a conversation is really important, as most media interviews are, stand up. Smile when appropriate. Your voice will sound warmer. You'll stay more focused and use more gestures. The reporter will hear your animated body language in your voice. The radio audience will hear it, too. And while the newspaper audience won't hear or see the actual "you," the print reporter will make decisions about you and your credibility which will color the story.

Microphone Manners

On Camera. Respect the microphone but let the reporter control it. He or she will place it where it needs to be. You don't need to lean down to it, nor should you grab it when the reporter extends it to you. If it's a lavaliere (clip-on) mike, the crew will put it in the proper location to pick up your voice. And always remember that any microphone may be live at any time and capable of transmitting your voice.

On Radio. When a radio reporter interviews you in the field, follow the same rules listed above for on camera interviews. Let the reporter control the microphone. However, when you are being interviewed in a radio studio, the microphone is stationary, usually hanging down in front of you. The host or engineer will help you adjust it so that it is about 6 inches from your mouth. Talk directly into the microphone.

Chapter Six

At News Conferences. Follow this additional rule: carefully observe where the microphones have been placed and don't walk out of their range when you are speaking.

Speeches. Test the microphone ahead of time. Locate the on-off switch. Don't tap it or blow into the microphone to test it. Adjust the microphone about six inches from your mouth so that you don't need to lean down to it. Talk directly into it. Speak in a normal voice to achieve the proper volume.

If you wish to move away from the lectern during your presentation, ask for a lavaliere (clip-on) mike with a long cord. It frees you to use gestures and to work with slides or overheads. If a lavaliere isn't available, request a stick mike with a long cord which will give you the freedom to leave the lectern. (A wireless mic is even better.)

Chapter 7

Media Interviews: Up Close and Sparkling

The interview is the bread and butter program for the media. Whether done on television, radio or in print, it is the best way of celebrating media's power to communicate. Every job holder in our society is in one sense an authority on interviews for he or she has passed at least one. But the coming together of interviewer and interviewee in the three major media categories presents for both a major challenge. The quality of the performance will be measured by a critical and demanding audience who have immediate judgmental power: in television, with the remote control; in radio, with the on-off knob; in print, with the turning of their eyes to another story.

In the thousands of interviews in which I have participated as interviewer, listener or reader, a few commonsense principles prevail. Here are a few general guides to prepare you to deal successfully in each particular interview situation you may face.

212

Chapter Seven

News Conferences

A news conference brings together in one place at the same time reporters from all interested TV stations, radio stations and newspapers. Good, competitive reporters generally don't like news conferences because everybody comes away with the same story. But for spokespersons, news conferences are efficient. Rather than spending all day giving interviews to four television stations, five radio stations and three newspapers, an organization or business can do the interviews all at once at a news conference.

Tips for Success. Reporters are "gun shy" about news conferences. Most have attended numerous news conferences called by publicity seekers or organizations who have no real news to convey. Make sure your proposed announcement is worthy of reporters making the time and effort to attend. Consider whether you can give out the information adequately in other ways such as a news release, phone calls or individual interviews. Once you "cry wolf" by calling a news conference and not delivering as promised, reporters will be unlikely to come back a second time.

If a subject is controversial, consider carefully whether to hold a news conference. When a group of reporters gathers, mob mentality may take over. The taste of blood puts the sharks in a feeding frenzy. As they show off for each other

SoundBites

how mean they can be, you may become the victim. If you expect a stormy session, plan the news conference so you can remain in control. Announce in advance that you have only a few minutes to spend with the media and that you and they will proceed best if reporters raise their hands before asking a question. Whatever occurs, never lose your temper.

Select the time and location of your news conference with an eye to publication schedules. If you want the news to break on the noon newscasts and in the afternoon paper, schedule the conference for 9:30 or 10:00 in the morning. If you want the news to be broadcast first on the evening newscasts and in the morning paper, schedule the conference for 1:30 or 2:00 in the afternoon.

Try to find a location which adds an interesting visual backdrop to your topic. Make sure there's adequate parking at the site — the closer to the conference the better. When holding the news conference inside, choose a room large enough for TV crews to set up their cameras and lights, but not so large that the audience seems lost in a cavernous space.

Make sure there are electrical outlets available. If you are holding the news conference outside, make sure ambient noise won't interfere. If possible, have a central sound system that TV and radio crews can plug into. Otherwise, expect that each station will need to place a microphone on the table or lectern in front of the spokesperson.

Chapter Seven

Notify the media at least a day in advance about your news conference. Don't try to be mysterious or vague about the topic. You have to sell the idea to the editor because there may not be enough staff to gamble on a dubious story idea. Understand that even though media outlets say they plan to send someone, circumstances can quickly change if a breaking news story occurs or a crew's camera breaks down.

You may include more than one spokesperson at your news conference, but it's best to limit the number. Three is maximum in most circumstances. When there is more than one person talking, it's best to stand up so whoever is addressing the audience can move in front of the microphones.

Hand out a written statement along with a news release or press packet to reporters as they arrive. Don't read a lengthy statement aloud to the audience. You'll quickly see their eyes glaze over. Instead, summarize your position (without reading) then offer to answer questions. Print reporters don't need to hear you read a statement because they have the written information in front of them. The TV and radio crews prefer recording off-the-cuff comments that are more natural.

Bring along visual aids which support your announcement. Charts, graphs, pictures and props help the reporters to understand and tell your story. Suggest other video TV crews can shoot to accompany the story.

Plan to stay after the news conference.

SoundBites

Some reporters may arrive late and will need to get additional information. Others will have a different angle they want to pursue. They don't want to tip off their competitors by asking questions in front of the entire audience.

Television Interviews

Taped TV News Story. The interview that is to be a part of a TV newscast is usually done on location by a mobile television news crew. Network news departments and news departments at larger stations send a reporter and/or producer, a videographer (what a TV photographer is sometimes called) and a sound person. Smaller stations send a reporter or producer and videographer. In a crunch situation, due to limitations of staff or time, a station may send only a videographer.

No matter how long you talk, your taped interview will be heavily edited into soundbites. Different soundbites may be selected for different news programs. Reporters may use one or several of your soundbites in each story. On the other hand, for various reasons (such as the slant of the story changed, you didn't provide enough cogent information, or time forced the story to be cut drastically), you might not appear at all in the newscast.

While the crew is at your location interviewing you, they may also want to get cover video of pertinent activities to go with their story.

Chapter Seven

Tips for Success. Accept that your story will not be told in depth. TV news stories generally run only a minute to a minute and a half. Prepare carefully to focus on the two or three main points you want stressed in the story. In your preparation, come up with and rehearse a couple of catchy soundbites that you can plant in your answers. Compose a one-sheet summary of your story the reporter can take back to the station. Be ready to steer the crew to a comfortable location for you to do the interview. Plan ahead of time for them to shoot cover video at your location if they should wish to do so. Further your cause by picking positive visuals for them to focus on. Be receptive and positive, but always keep your agenda in mind.

One big advantage of a taped interview which will be edited: you can stop and start over if you make a mistake. Don't make a big deal about it. Just calmly pause and say, "I misspoke... let me start over," or, "I lost my train of thought. could you ask the question again?"

Live TV News Story. Television news values the "immediate." That's why stations generally have at least one "live shot" during a broadcast, and sometimes many more. The live interview is conducted during a newscast on location by a reporter. It is often done in conjunction with a breaking news story such as a fire or accident, but can also include feature and general news subjects. Stations frequently put their weather person on location at an event to give that static segment more flavor than is possible inside a sterile studio. During his or her segment, the weather person may interview people at the scene.

Stations regularly contrive the appearance of live television by putting a reporter on location to simply introduce and wrap up a pre-packaged story. This "Sony sandwich," as it is called in station jargon, carries much of the weight of a live TV presentation.

Technology has come a long way in the last few years. On major breaking stories every station in town may have a live truck and crew at your location vying to interview you at the top of their newscast. By satellite, they can also send stories back to the station from any location in the world. It was satellite that permitted local stations around the country to send their own crews to cover such events as the O.J. Simpson trial, the Oklahoma City bombing, and the Mexico City earthquake.

Tips for Success. Plan your agenda with care in breadth and depth. Even though your statements will be unedited, they must be of soundbite potency. Your time on the air will be your actual time on the air. Every second before the camera will be seen and heard by the audience.

These facts concerning your performance may be intimidating, but by forethought you can make the interview yours. Mentally, by focusing on your agenda, you can shut out any distractions on the scene such as traffic, people milling around, or the crew working behind the camera. You and your agenda are on the stage. The performance is underway. This can be your moment of achievement.

Live On Set. Rarely will the television news department invite you to be live on set with the anchors during the newscast. Occasionally, though, to vary the pace and look of the newscast, to boost the credibility of the anchors, or to honor an important expert, the news producer will ask a guest to sit on the news set to be interviewed by the anchor people. For example, a political commentator may discuss the candidates during election coverage, the governor might be invited to talk about his plan to reduce crime, or an expert on Israel may be asked to give her opinions on the latest peace initiatives.

Tips for Success. Prepare as you normally would for a television interview by reviewing your intimate knowledge of the subject and focusing on your agenda. Get to the studio early so you can orient yourself and see where you'll be sitting. Speak to the producer ahead of time and to the anchors if they're available. Discuss with them how and when you will get on and off the set so as not to disrupt the newscast. Adjust yourself to the lighting circumstances: TV lights may seem hot and blinding. Learn who will put on your microphone and when, and generally familiarize yourself with the specifics of the newscast in which you are to participate.

SoundBites

TV Interview Show. Interview shows, or talk shows, have become a staple of television. In general, the interview is done in a studio setting with one or two hosts talking to one or more guests. The format is called "live on tape," which means the program is recorded as if it is being done live, then played back at a later time. In many instances there may be a studio audience that participates in the program.

When we think of talk on TV, a wide range of syndicated and network shows comes to mind. There are the sensationalized ones such as those hosted by Geraldo Rivera, Sally Jessy Raphael, and Ricki Lake. More conventional daytime talk hosts include Oprah Winfrey and Phil Donahue (now off the air). Other hosts' programs tackle more traditional topics: Larry King, David Frost, Tim Russert. Then there are interview shows labeled as specials such those by Barbara Walters and Diane Sawyer.

But local stations can also have their own TV interview shows or public affairs programs. These vary greatly in scope and quality. Many of the best focus on important issues in the community and afford excellent opportunities for political and business leaders to communicate with their constituencies.

Tips for Success. The famous Boy Scout motto, "Be prepared," never rang with sounder resonance than in talk television. Because of the length and depth of these types of interviews, you must plan well if you are to achieve a credible performance. Your expertise will frequently be the reason for your invitation to appear. Your pre-show thinking and rehearsal may make the difference between success and failure.

If you are one of several guests on talk television, you must be prepared to deal openly, graciously, yet steadfastly, with those who disagree with you or who want to use you to advance their own agenda. Preparation and forethought can be loyal guard dogs in talk TV.

Review the advice for studio appearances given above for live on set interviews.

Anchor Interview. During an anchor interview, you and the interviewer are in different locations talking to each other through cameras and ear pieces. For example, on *Nightline,* Ted Koppel talks from his studio location to people all over the world who appear in boxes on the screen. Others such as Katie Couric and Matt Lauer on the *Today Show* use the same technique.

The anchor interview is occasionally done by local news operations. They'll send a photographer without a reporter to your location, as well as a live truck and crew. Then, during the newscast, an anchorperson in the studio asks you questions you receive through an ear piece.

Tips for Success. The special challenge of a TV anchor interview is having to look directly into the camera as you receive questions, formulate your response, and speak. When you're accustomed to talking to people, responding to their facial expressions and gestures, you may find the camera a cold receptor. To be yourself and overcome the difficulties of meeting the camera's eye, the inexperienced interviewee should practice. That practice will be complete the day of the interview when you make sure the ear piece stays in place and is comfortable.

The interview is unedited and gives you an opportunity to certify by gesture and facial expression the validity of your message.

Print Interviews

Newspaper Story/Magazine Story. Interviews for newspapers and magazines vary greatly. The most important are done in person. Many are done by telephone. Lengthy interviews may be done over several days or weeks. If you are to be interviewed, ascertain the deadline against which your interviewer is working. For daily newspapers, deadlines are usually tight. For newspaper features, investigative pieces, or special sections, reporters may have several days or weeks to do a story. Weekly newspapers set their deadlines a couple of days before publication (for instance, Thursday for Saturday distribution). Magazines stories must be finished well in advance of publication, whether the periodical is a weekly, a monthly or a quarterly.

Chapter Seven

Tips for Success. Take advantage of the scope that a newspaper or magazine interview allows. Plan your agenda in breadth and depth, and with the knowledge that what you say is to appear in permanent form where it will be read and examined through time. As the interview progresses, make sure the reporter understands the fine distinctions you are making because of your detailed knowledge of your subject. Shape your answers to contain interesting quotes the reporter is likely to use. If it is telephone interview, don't get too comfortable or folksy — don't spill confidences to an eager reporter. Keep in mind, in any print interview, the reporter may be recording you, often without your knowledge. Do consider making your own tape of a print interview to have a record for critiquing and improving your performance.

Editorial Board Meeting. Talking to a
newspaper's editorial board allows you to fully explain an important issue in the news, one which the publication will be covering and which may generate an editorial opinion. When you call or write to suggest a meeting, your request will be judged on it's timeliness, importance, and whether there is a need for clarification. If your request is granted, personnel attending may include the editor, the editorial page editor, an editorial writer, a reporter who covers the issue involved and the editor of the relevant newspaper section (such as the business editor).

SoundBites

Tips for Success. Resist the temptation to bring your entire entourage to the meeting with you — take only one or two key people. While the atmosphere may be friendly and casual, don't let that lull you into making unguarded statements. Be warm and personable, but remember that everything you say at an editorial board meeting is on the record. Your information and quotes may be used in a story immediately following the meeting or can appear at any time in the future. The meeting will usually last for 45 minutes to an hour. Plan to use the first five to ten minutes for some introductory comments — using notes but without reading verbatim — then let editors ask questions for the balance of the time.

Radio Interviews

Radio Talk Show. Of all talk shows, those on radio are most truly pure talk. They thrive because human beings have found the human voice the most enduring way of our touching and negotiating openly with our fellow human beings. If you are interviewed on radio, you may well speak from your home or office, or be interviewed in the studio. You may be invited to engage with an unseen audience, many of whom will voice strong opinions on almost any topic. The host or hosts of the show may interview you live or on tape for later playback.

Chapter Seven

Tips for Success. Being a largely vocal medium, radio takes the emphasis off personal appearance but increases emphasis on vocal performance. Participating in it, you can be comfortable because it doesn't matter how you look or what you're wearing. These circumstances, however, are not an invitation for sloppy thinking or lazy preparation. By their nature and length, radio permits in-depth examination of important issues. Its audience runs the gamut of the general population; you will be heard in cars, at home, in offices, wherever sound can fill a space.

Although your statements will go unedited, you can and should be prepared to respond to almost anything because of the freewheeling nature of radio interviewing where listeners call in to participate. In recent times, some radio talk show hosts have become performers who thrive on the outrageous. Others have strong personal and political views that color their exchanges with interviewees. Prepare yourself for the kinds of questions and challenges such hosts may offer.

Taped Radio Interview/Live Radio Interview.
The taped radio interview is done over the telephone or by a reporter in person with a portable recorder. The interview typically is edited into soundbites for use in scheduled newscasts throughout the day.

Live radio interviews, usually of a softer nature, may be done by disc jockeys and other hosts during regular programming. During a breaking story, short interviews may be done live by phone or in person during the radio newscast. Often these are extremely crucial issues demanding utmost judgment.

Tips for Success. In radio interviewing, be alert. A reporter may call when you least expect it and begin taping or interviewing you live immediately. When engaged on the telephone, you must remember at all times that you are being recorded. If you negotiate the interview and buy yourself time, you will have a much better opportunity to advance your agenda.

Interviews in Cyberspace

Media relations online — including interviewing — is ever evolving. While freelance reporters and those from trade publications are more likely to use the Internet for research, to find sources, receive press releases and conduct interviews, many mainstream reporters at newspapers, TV and radio stations have not made the transition. They still seem comfortable doing business the old fashioned way — by phone, by FAX, by mail and in person.

If you agree to be interviewed in cyberspace, a reporter will usually send you a list of questions by E-mail. You can then carefully craft your answers before E-mailing them back to the reporter.

Chapter Seven

Tips for Success. Interviewing online appeals to those who like utmost control in their interviews. Every answer can be thoughtfully scripted. Because the reporter has in writing everything you said, he or she has no excuse not to quote your exact words. On the other hand, some people are troubled by the prospect of answering questions online because they lose the give and take of a conversation. Interviewees can't confirm that the reporter understands their messages. They can't expand on and further clarify ideas. And they may be at a disadvantage because they can't judge through the reporter's tone of voice what his or her slant is on the story.

If you decide to grant an online interview, the basic rules of interviewing apply. Identify your key messages, then work them into each answer. Even though you are writing your answers, you must still follow the five C's to be quotable: keep your answers clear, concise, conversational, catchy and colorful.

For those of you who participate in online forums, be aware that messages you post there may also be fair game for a journalist looking for sources and quotes on a particular subject.

Post-Interview Evaluation

After you have experienced an interview using the techniques and tips in this guide, take time to evaluate how well you did. If you taped

SoundBites

the interview, review it as well as your copy of the finished story. Determine whether there are areas which still need practice or improvement.

Use the following checklist to help you evaluate how you performed in the interview:

Follow-Up Checklist

Reporter's name_____

Station or publication_____

Style/attitude of reporter_____
_____

Date of interview_____

Date story ran_____

Location_____

Topic of the story_____

Format of finished story (talk show, feature, etc.)
_____
_____

Length of finished story_____
_____

Chapter Seven

Were you prepared?_____

_____

_____

Did you convey all your messages? Which
ones?_____

_____

Which of your messages were used?_____

_____

_____

What soundbites or quotes were used? Did you
want them to be used?_____

_____

_____

Did you fall into any traps? (Repeating negatives,
getting defensive, saying too much,
etc.)_____

_____

What will you do differently the next
time?_____

_____

_____

Chapter 8

Confronting Crises

Human history records crisis after crisis writ large. Reading it with care and reflecting on our own lives, you and I surmise crisis is endemic to the human condition. Smiling wryly, we may take some relief from a soundbite of biblical wisdom in the book of Job: "Man is born unto trouble as the sparks fly upward." Coming closer to home we may recall Murphy's law: "Whatever can go wrong, will go wrong." Again we smile, grit our teeth and murmur: "Crisis, crisis go away; come again some other day." But our mirror image tells us: "This is the other day, and the only way to deal with crisis is to prepare for it." Easier said than done, but let's have a go at it.

Facing crisis is not new for individuals, companies, organizations, and governments. What is new is that because of advances in technology and communication, crises no longer happen in private. Mistakes in crisis management that have not reckoned with the pervasiveness of the news media and the importance of public opinion — those forces with which this book deals — have devastated thousands of people and have seriously damaged or destroyed countless companies and organizations.

But just a bit more background here. In

Chapter Eight

Greek the word *krisis* means *decision*. If we define crisis as a major unforeseen occurrence or happening, the Greek root of the word takes on great significance: MANAGERS WHO ASSESS THE SCOPE AND PROBABLE FARTHEST REACH OF THE HAPPENING AND DEAL WITH IT OPENLY AND DECISIVELY ARE LIKELY TO HANDLE IT WELL. With planning and practice, good leaders do whatever is required, placing human values above monetary values, but generally preserving both. In most organizations, such planning and practice will entail mock runthroughs including communications sessions as carefully crafted as are annual reports, stockholders meetings and production procedures or major sales campaigns. In short, crisis management demands special programming and is likely to test managers in ways not taught in most business schools.

Let's examine two masterful politicians of our era and the way they responded to crises. Franklin Delano Roosevelt, who was to become our 32nd President and the only one elected for four terms, at the age of 39 suffered a severe attack of poliomyelitis that left his right leg paralyzed. A personal crisis that had to be dealt with every day of his life, it was accepted by him as a burden to be borne. Humanized and matured beyond his years by his suffering, he faced a second major crisis — public not private — when he assumed the presidency on March 4, 1933, with the nation trapped in the Great Depression

231

SoundBites

brought on by the stock market crash of 1929. Speaking as one equal to any challenge he assured the stricken nation that we had nothing to fear but fear itself, adding that his would be a leadership drawing on "the support and understanding of the people themselves" offered "in every dark hour of our national life."

A similar awareness and cultivation of public sentiment marked his response to the crisis brought on by Japan's surprise devastation of our Pacific fleet at Pearl Harbor on December 7, 1941. Even though historians contend that Roosevelt's conduct of domestic and foreign policy may have been "devious if not dishonest," they all acknowledge that throughout his political career he made exemplary use of modern media to make sure public sentiment endorsed his every action.

How different — and informing — the career of Richard Milhous Nixon, our 37th President, as he responded to crises. Named as Vice President on the 1952 Republican ticket headed by General Dwight David Eisenhower, but charged with having created an $18,000 slush fund to promote his political career, Nixon went on national television September 23, 1952, and successfully defended himself in his famous "Checkers Speech" detailing his family finances in almost embarrassing openness. Contending that his wife, Pat, possessed no fur coat but wore a "respectable Republican cloth coat" and that he intended to keep the cocker spaniel Checkers, which was a political gift to his daughters,

Chapter Eight

Nixon engaged public sentiment so fully that Eisenhower felt compelled to keep him on the ticket, and did so through two administrations that opened the door to Nixon's election to the presidency in his own right.

Two decades later, then-President Nixon apparently forgot the crisis management skills which had earlier saved his political career. When the scandal associated with the White House engineered break-in at the Democratic headquarters in the Watergate complex occurred, Nixon was neither open nor forthcoming. In actions later revealed on tapes meant to establish his place in history, he scrambled to cover up his involvement even if it meant sacrificing friends and associates. In appearance after appearance he stonewalled the public and the press, refusing to be accountable, refusing to apologize. In 1974, facing almost certain trial and conviction in impeachment proceedings before the U.S. Senate, he resigned the presidency, the first man in our two hundred year history to do so. Whether better crisis management skills might have saved this gifted politician, we will never know, but certainly the actions taken by Nixon prove the price of defying public sentiment.

From Bad to Worse

Exxon. In public relations circles, the *Exxon Valdez* disaster has become the classic example of poor crisis management and the detrimental long term effects those bad decisions can cause. Just after midnight on March 24, 1989, the supertanker *Valdez* was filled to its capacity of 53 million gallons of oil at the Alyeska pipeline terminal in the port of Valdez, Alaska. As the huge, 987 foot freighter moved through scenic Prince William Sound, it ran aground on Bligh Reef, tearing a hole in the hull which penetrated 11 of 17 cargo tanks. Within five hours, more than 10 million gallons of oil had gushed from the damaged freighter, at that time the largest spill ever in U.S. waters. Ever widening, the black slick eventually spread across 3,000 square miles of ocean, destroying sea birds and sea life, ruining spawning grounds and fish hatcheries.

Although Exxon's cleanup began the afternoon after the accident, many people wondered why more wasn't done to limit the spill as it occurred. While Exxon received most of the blame, the Alyeska Pipeline Service Company (a joint venture of seven companies, including Exxon) was also found at fault. The company's response vessel had been damaged in a wind storm so it couldn't be used to help contain the spill. Experts believe that after loading more than 8,000 successful cargoes, Alyeska employees had become complacent about safety.

No company could have come out of such an environmental disaster unscathed, but Exxon exacerbated the problem by not communicating clearly about its actions and by creating the perception that it was less than totally concerned about the horrible damage it caused. Even though

Chapter Eight

Exxon spokespersons held regular news conferences in Alaska during the height of the crisis, top executives in New York refused comment for almost a week. When they did talk, they appeared to be almost complacent; *The New York Times* quoted one official as saying the damage to the environment was "minimal." Lawrence Rawl, the chairman of Exxon, didn't travel to Alaska himself until three weeks after the spill, further perpetuating the idea that the company wasn't truly concerned about the human and monetary costs of their disaster.

Fueled by media reports and pictures of dead wildlife on the 6 p.m. news, public opinion vilified Exxon. People vowed to boycott the company's gas stations, while others returned their cut-up credit cards. Two years after the accident, Exxon agreed to pay 900 million dollars to settle civil suits brought because of the spill and another 100 million in fines. CEO Rawl, apparently trying to reassure stockholders, said, "The settlement will have no noticeable effect on our financial results." The public again became infuriated with what they perceived as his lack of remorse. Rawl — and his company — again came in for scathing criticism from the media, the public, and government officials. An executive who had been considered a star in his industry, Lawrence Rawl will now be most remembered for the *Valdez* crisis. And the negative public opinion of his conduct during the Exxon crisis seems likely to last for decades.

SoundBites

NASA. For 28 years, NASA had a reputation as one of the most effective self-promoters in Washington. Since its creation in 1958, the agency had carefully crafted its image by managing the flow of information to stimulate public and political support. It depended heavily on the media to tell those stories and had basked in the limelight of 24 successful space shuttle launches. For weeks leading up to the launch of the shuttle Challenger on January 28, 1986, NASA experienced some of its best publicity ever. The media was captivated by a new twist on shuttle travel: Challenger would carry the first civilian into space, New Hampshire master teacher Christa McAuliffe. Even President Reagan appeared on TV trumpeting Challenger's undertaking.

Then the crisis. On the morning of the launch, excitement turned to horror as people around the country — including children in their classrooms — watched the shuttle explode just after liftoff, obviously killing all seven aboard. Besides confirming that the shuttle had blown up (which millions of people saw with their own eyes live on national television), NASA refused to talk to reporters for five hours after the explosion. Even the weather report became a secret. Reporters questioning a National Weather Service official in Miami were referred to a nearby Air Force base. In what became a crisis management disaster, NASA impounded all the weather data collected before, during, and after the launch.

After decades of witnessing NASA's slick

Chapter Eight

promotion and apparent media savvy, reporters were surprised at the agency's silent "no comment" in the wake of the tragedy. The lack of information created a dangerous vacuum. Silence fueled rumors spread by so-called experts who speculated on what had happened. The disaster was attributed to everything from foreign sabotage to a puncture in the external fuel tank. Reporters sought other sources, some of whom leaked information damaging to NASA. During the subsequent investigation, several NASA officials contradicted one another on safety and operating procedures. Now we rightfully ask: How could NASA have been so ill prepared?

Ironically, we now know that NASA had a crisis plan which emphasized the importance of making a public statement within 20 minutes of an accident. But after so many years of unblemished accomplishment, the space agency was clearly caught off guard. NASA had been spoiled by success. Its "can't fail" attitude at the moment of crisis exacerbated its failure. A major human and technological tragedy became a public relations fiasco that severely damaged the agency's prestige and credibility.

Jack in the Box. On January 11, 1993, 2-year-old Michael Nole happily devoured the cheeseburger bought for him at the Jack in the Box restaurant on South 56th Street in Tacoma, Washington. The next night he was rushed to Children's Hospital and Medical Center in Seattle with severe stomach cramps and bloody diarrhea.

SoundBites

Ten days later, Michael died of kidney and heart failure.

By then numerous crisis reports had begun pouring into the San Diego headquarters of Jack in the Box's parent, Foodmaker Inc. Nearly 300 people had been stricken with the same *E. coli* bacteria responsible for Michael's death, apparently after eating at Jack in the Box outlets in Idaho, Nevada, and Washington, or after coming in contact with restaurant customers.

The crisis team worked from a plan devised in the mid-1980's. It quickly ordered the destruction of 20,000 pounds of hamburger patties prepared at meat plants where the deadly *E coli* bacteria was suspected of originating. It changed meat suppliers, installed a toll-free number to field consumer complaints, and instructed employees to turn up the cooking heat to kill the deadly bacteria.

All these planned-for remedial responses were exactly what needed to be done, but the company's poor communications about what it was doing undermined its actions and caused Jack in the Box to suffer in public esteem. The company appeared uncaring about its victims. Because tracing the source of *E coli* can be difficult, it took nearly a week for the company to admit publicly its responsibility for the poisonings, apologize to the families, and offer to pay all medical bills. And even those actions when they came seemed half-hearted to many observers. At a Seattle news conference, the Jack in the Box president appeared less than open about the occurrence. He criticized health officials for not telling the company about new cooking regulations and blamed the company's major meat supplier.

Shareholders, franchisees, and victims filed class action suits against Jack in the Box. In July, parents of the victims claimed the company failed to pay medical bills as promised. Negative press continued for more than a year after the crisis. As a result, Jack in the Box reported a $44 million loss in 1993 after a $22 million profit in 1992. Its stock fell 43%.

What more could Jack in the Box have done? Had the company taken responsible action based on its 1980's crisis plan, it would not have appeared unconcerned and inept. Moreover, the restaurant chain could have extended immediately the apologetic ads it ran in Seattle to other important cities such as Los Angeles.

The company could have softened the negative impact by immediately showing compassion for victims and their families, and making it clear that people were the company's first priority. Some crisis experts suggest the company should have closed every store for a week or more for a thorough inspection, a strategy which would have dramatized the company's concern. Compassion could have reduced negative media coverage, convinced more families to settle claims faster, saved Jack in the Box stock from taking such a steep dive, and curbed shareholder and franchisee suits. Most of all, Jack in the Box would have enhanced its reputation as a family-oriented restaurant chain that put human values before financial cares.

TWA. Trans World Airlines CEO, Jeffrey Erickson, was awakened on July 17,1996 at 2 a.m. London time with the call every airline executive dreads. Flight 800 carrying 230 passengers and crew from New York to Paris had exploded shortly after takeoff from Kennedy Airport. Witnesses reported seeing a fireball, then flaming pieces of the 747 falling into the ocean. Immediately people speculated that a bomb had been planted on board the plane or that it had been attacked by a missile. Rescuers and private citizens rushed to their boats to try to rescue survivors, but it soon became apparent that all had perished.

For obvious reasons, every airline has a crash crisis management plan. But Erickson, a veteran airline executive who had also worked at Reno Air and Aloha Airgroup, had never experienced a major crash on his watch. After getting the news about Flight 800, he and a public relations executive with him in London immediately chartered a private plane, but still the two of them didn't get back to New York until 13 hours after the crash. The fact that Erickson and a communications specialist were in London on business instead of three hours away in the company's St. Louis headquarters was only one of a series of bad luck coincidences that hampered TWA's response to the crisis.

Chapter Eight

There was also a dearth of managers who were available to respond in Erickson's absence. Two top people — the marketing vice president and CFO — had resigned a month earlier. In fact, many TWA managers in St. Louis were attending a going away party for one of the former executives when the chorus of beepers announced the terrible tragedy off Long Island.

Logistics were also difficult. As a smaller airline, TWA's trauma team — made up of 650 employee volunteers — was scattered across the country. Larger carriers have regional response teams. Getting the whole TWA team to New York ate up precious hours.

To make matters worse, New York Mayor Rudolph Giuliani set up camp at Kennedy Airport, blasting the airline for its "abysmal and horrible" performance in notifying the victims' relatives. TWA then got into a battle of words with Giuliani, making the airline look defensive.

The spokesperson by default during the first hours after the crash until CEO Erickson and others arrived was Mike Kelly, Vice President of operations at New York's Kennedy Airport. In live on-air appearances through the night he seemed unprepared and disorganized, and less than effectual in conveying compassion, the most important element of any crisis response where people have been injured or killed. Granted, Kelly was not a communications professional, but one wonders why had he not been media trained to handle a crisis situation. Even with people out of town and others resigning, TWA should have had a trained spokesperson ready to talk to the media in the event of a crisis. Critics claim other communications suffered as well. On-duty personnel at TWA reportedly acted callous toward grieving family members, and calls from the media went unanswered.

When Erickson finally arrived from London, *The New York Times* noted that he looked unprepared and cut short a news conference, refusing to answer questions. In retrospect, it would have seemed reasonable for Erickson to hold a quick satellite news conference from London before heading to New York or at least call to make a statement from his plane.

Actually, many people praised TWA for its actions after the initial slow response. Families were all notified within 23 hours after the crash, which is considered fairly fast by industry standards. But in a crisis, doing something isn't enough. Companies have to communicate what they're doing because oftentimes perception becomes as important as reality, and helps determine it.

The Good Get Better Faster

Tylenol. If Exxon stands as the classic example in PR circles of what not to do in a crisis, Johnson & Johnson's management of the Tylenol poisonings in 1982 represents a lesson in decisiveness, compassion, and effective damage control under most difficult conditions. Indeed, what

Chapter Eight

Johnson & Johnson did about its Tylenol crisis has become the standard against which other companies' crisis management is judged.

Johnson & Johnson got its first hint of trouble the morning of September 30, 1982. A reporter from the Chicago *Tribune*, investigating a death the day before, called the company's PR office. He said the Chicago medical examiner believed there was a link between the man's death and Tylenol. Then the crisis exploded. Within two days, a total of seven people had died after taking Extra-Strength Tylenol capsules tainted with cyanide. While no one has ever been arrested for the tamperings, James Lewis was convicted for trying to extort $2 million from Johnson & Johnson and is serving 20 years in federal prison. He's denied any involvement in the tampering, but some investigators believe he was the person responsible for the murders.

After the deaths in Chicago, Tylenol sales dropped by 87 percent. Stressing its concern for the public, and fearing that something had gone wrong in one of its plants, Johnson & Johnson acted swiftly and decisively by recalling and destroying 22 million bottles of Tylenol at a cost of $100 million. The company quickly launched constant and correct communication. It set up an 800 number so customers, law enforcement agencies and others could get information directly from J & J. It also regularly communicated to employees about the status of the crisis with videos, meetings, and newsletters.

Throughout the crisis, Johnson & Johnson

SoundBites

received 2500 media inquiries. While the main thrust of the stories was about the poisoning victims and the police investigation, during and after the crisis many reporters also commented on the company's polished public relations offensive. A seven-member J & J strategy group met twice daily in Chairman James Burke's office during the first six weeks of the crisis. Burke himself was available and open with the media including appearances on national television programs such as the *Phil Donahue Show* and *60 Minutes*. J &J was able to collect on some of the good will it had put in the bank by establishing beneficial relationships with media over the years.

After the recall and the discovery that the poison had not been put into the Tylenol during manufacturing, Johnson & Johnson realized what *its* real crisis was: could it save the Tylenol brand, which before the poisonings had 35 percent of the over-the-counter pain reliever market? The company immediately went to work on tamper-resistant packaging which it introduced to the world at a 30-city teleconference on November 11th. By the end of the year, just three months after the first victim died, Tylenol regained nearly all the market share it had before the crisis.

Surprisingly, Johnson & Johnson had no labeled crisis management plan in place when the Tylenol crisis occurred. But J & J did have a written plan of sorts which Chairman James Burke and company managers followed all along without knowing it. That plan was Johnson & Johnson's Credo which says the company has

Chapter Eight

four responsibilities in this order: 1. To consumers, 2. To employees, 3. To the communities they serve, 4. To stockholders. By being open and decisive, and setting human and monetary values in proper perspective, J & J saved Tylenol. With the Tylenol crisis behind it, J & J was and still is viewed as a responsible citizen.

Pepsi. A more recent product tampering crisis turned out to be a hoax, but Pepsi-Cola still faced the possibility of serious repercussions to its business. The crisis hit during a key time of the year for soft drink sales — just before the Fourth of July holiday, 1993. On June 9, a man in Tacoma, Washington, claimed to have found a syringe in a can of Diet Pepsi. After that report hit the media, another call came from the same area. By June 14, the company had received eight more complaints of tainted Pepsi, and by June 23, more than 50 calls from around the country.

Pepsi faced a grave crisis, but it had a clearly defined crisis management plan. The Pepsi crisis team responded quickly. When the networks began calling the day after the first report, Pepsi was ready with its response: video footage showing cans whizzing at 30 mph down the production line at a bottling plant, demonstrating how it's virtually impossible to insert a syringe or anything else into cans during the one second they remain open for filling and capping. Pepsi immediately made the video available by satellite to any station that wanted to use it.

SoundBites

CEO Craig Weatherup of Pepsi-Cola North America appeared on the morning and evening network news shows as well as *The MacNeil/Lehrer Newshour* and *Larry King Live,* explaining how a syringe could never get into a Pepsi can. In addition, the company was able to link up effectively with FDA commissioner David Kessler. They presented a united front. Kessler supported Pepsi's claims that there had been no nationwide tampering and that there was no need for a recall.

The company communicated to other key audiences. Every morning during the week of the crisis, employees received an update from CEO Weatherup. The consumer relations group got new information at least once a day so they could answer the thousands of calls that came into the company's 800 number. Salespeople in the field were also briefed continuously so they could talk to customers.

Because of the company's swift action and constant communication, consumer research the week of the crisis showed that 94 percent of the people who were aware of the stories felt that Pepsi was responding in a responsible way. To formally close the issue, the company ran a national newspaper ad declaring: "Pepsi is pleased to announce . . . nothing." Yet the crisis did hurt. Pepsi lost $10 to $15 million in sales in that one week. Luckily, it happened at the beginning of a hot, thirsty summer. With effective and ready crisis management, sales rebounded two weeks after the scare.

Chapter Eight

Ashland Oil. A year before the *Exxon Valdez* crisis, another oil spill received very different media coverage. On January 2, 1988, workers at an Ashland Oil facility in Floreffe, Pennsylvania were filling a huge storage tank with diesel fuel. It was a routine operation except that the container was being filled for the first time since having been cut up, moved from Cleveland and reconstructed on the site near the Monongahela River. The 48 foot structure was almost filled to its four million gallon capacity when something went wrong. The tank collapsed, spilling its contents in a matter of seconds. Much of the oil poured into the Monongahela and headed for Pittsburgh, 23 miles downstream. Within 24 hours, 23,000 people in the metro area found themselves without tap water and 750,000 others were forced to ration their drinking water. Thousands of families were evacuated, dozens of factories had to shut down, schools were closed and commercial traffic on the river was halted.

Within days, because of unusually swift currents, the oil had flowed from the Monongahela into the Ohio River all the way down to Louisville, Kentucky threatening communities' water supplies along the way. Because it was the middle of winter when plants are dormant, fish are inactive and birds have flown south, damage to the rivers' ecosystems was not as devastating as it would have been in summer. Even so, the spill killed 2,000 birds and 11,000 fish.

Despite the severity of the spill and the

extent of the damage, the media praised Ashland's quick response and openness. Ignoring legal advice, CEO John Hall flew to Pittsburgh to apologize and admit the company had made mistakes. Ashland had not gotten the proper permit for the rebuilt tank from county authorities. It had also forgone the usual safety practice of testing the tank with a full load of water.

But CEO Hall practiced successful crisis management. In addition to being open with the media, he immediately put Ashland employees to work cleaning up the damage. He hired contractors to survey the damage and provide additional cleanup. Ashland also alerted local, state, and federal authorities to bring them up to date and enlist their help. Top executives took the media and concerned officials on tours of the area and brought in temporary piping to provide communities with clean drinking water.

To maintain morale and contain rumors within the company, managers communicated to employees the company's actions throughout the crisis. It began its own investigation of the tank explosion and hired an outside firm to render an unbiased, factual report of what had occurred. Rather than trying to hide damaging reports, the company announced them publicly.

Ashland spent more than $13 million on the clean-up. It faced nearly two dozen class action suits and an indictment from the government for violating environmental laws. Yet in the court of public opinion, Ashland Oil succeeded where Exxon didn't. Ashland's response to crisis

Chapter Eight

was immediate, visual, and constant. Its actions showed its human and monetary values were properly prioritized.

Luby's. It was Tuesday, October 16, 1991. The usual lunchtime crowd jammed Luby's Cafeteria in Killeen, Texas. Suddenly a pickup truck barreled straight through the restaurant's plate-glass window. People thought it was a freak accident — until the driver jumped from behind the wheel with a semiautomatic pistol and began firing. "This is what Bell County did to me. This is payback day!" he shouted as he made his way through the restaurant, pumping bullets in every direction. The gunman, 35-year old George Hennard, an unemployed seaman with a reputation as an oddball, continued firing for ten minutes, until four police officers arrived on the scene. They returned his fire, wounding him several times. He stumbled into a rear alcove where he fired a bullet into his own head. Twenty three people — including Hennard — lay dead.

In San Antonio, the Luby's Cafeteria Inc. board of directors was meeting when word came that there had been a shooting at the restaurant in Killeen. Without knowing the extent of the problem, two corporate officers immediately left to drive the 175 miles to Killeen. When the company headquarters got an update that several people had been killed, CEO Pete Erben and a public relations executive left to fly to Killeen on a private jet. When they landed, the media rushed

SoundBites

for a comment. The executives spoke briefly about why they were there but said they didn't have much information yet. They then began contacting employees to check on injuries. They visited the family of one employee who was missing. (He was later found hiding in a dishwasher.)

CEO Erben established a primary crisis control center at the San Antonio headquarters and set up a Killeen communication center at a local motel. Luby's public relations people identified major audiences to contact: board members, insurance companies, Luby's other 150 units, government officials, etc. The company continuously communicated to the media with background on the corporation and whatever other information they could give.

The next morning, the managers met with employees and their families, assuring them that their incomes wouldn't be affected and that the company would provide any assistance they needed. The next meeting was a news conference with reporters.

After the crisis subsided, Erben said in an interview that communication was the essence of Luby's response. "You don't want to avoid the media," he said. "Be truthful to them, just tell what you know, don't speculate and don't hesitate to talk about your mission."

United Way. Financial mismanagement in business is bad enough, but a nonprofit organization depending on the generosity and good will of others can't afford even the hint of fiscal irre-

Chapter Eight

sponsibility. On February 16, 1992 the *Washington Post* broke such a story about the largest nonprofit agency in the U.S., United Way of America. The article accused the agency's president, William Aramony, of extravagant spending habits, including allegations that he had flown abroad on the Concorde, used expensive limousines, and took trips with his mistress — all with the charity's money. Aramony resigned on January 27, 1992 and ultimately was indicted for fraud.

Rocked by scandal, the national United Way as well as the 1000 local United Ways around the country began trying to salvage their upcoming fundraising campaigns. The national office had received advance warning that the *Washington Post* was ready to break the story, so the board of directors had already launched its own investigation using an outside firm. The PR staff had gone into action as well, setting up a hotline for the public and the media to use. Staff throughout the organization had been trained to answer questions. PR staff also faxed information regularly to the local offices, first warning them about the article, then continuing to keep them updated about the status of the investigation. They held teleconferences with 90 cities hooked in so local chapters could ask questions.

Two months after Aramony's resignation, the outside investigators presented to the United Way board their report and recommendations for organizational change. After being approved unanimously by the board, the United Way air-expressed the report to all the local offices.

SoundBites

At the same time, the local United Ways put their own crisis plans into action. Donors were angry. Some canceled pledges, others voiced serious concerns. The local offices realized their only strategy was to distance themselves from the national organization. Most reinforced the messages that they were community-based organizations, governed by local volunteers and providing support to local organizations.

The United Way weathered the storm: with constant communication to all audiences during and after the crisis; by installing internal audits and controls on hiring procedures, work practices, and officers' compensation; and by launching a PR blitz to show the public the value of services the charity provides and the importance of donors' dollars.

Planning for Crisis

When business is going well, it's hard to think about, let alone plan for, an unplanned event. But that's exactly when we should be thinking about and planning for the worst — when we can be calm and calculating, when we have the time to consider our options — *before* it hits the fan.

As much as we'd like to ignore and avoid the possibility, crisis can happen to any organization at any time. No one is immune. Those who strategize and prepare a written Crisis Management Plan (CMP) ahead of time are more likely to weather a crisis with their reputations intact.

Chapter Eight

Crisis Management Plan. A programmed Crisis Management Plan is like a flashlight in our home. The CMP is the first thing employees can grab to show them the way through the sudden confusion when a crisis occurs. It's much easier to locate the flashlight before we need it — when the sun is shining and the lights are working. The CMP is a confidential, limited circulation document that should be updated at least once a year to keep up with changes in the organization.

Assemble a Crisis Response Team. A team should be established to manage the crisis as it unfolds. Most crisis management experts suggest a small (ten or less), dynamic group which is representative of the company. The group may vary in composition depending on the nature of the crisis being addressed. Personnel to consider include the CEO or someone else in senior management, technical experts, a public relations professional, an attorney, someone from advertising, an investor relations person, an operations manager, a financial officer, and a public affairs expert. (Keep in mind that someone is going to have to be available to keep the company or organization running normally while the team is managing the crisis.)

Assess risks. Managers should do a "crisis audit" of the organization. A summary of potential disasters should then be included in the written CMP. Where is the organization most vulner-

SoundBites

able? What kinds of problems could occur? What crises have occurred to other companies in the industry? How likely are they to happen? If they do happen, how serious might they be?

Definitions of what actually constitutes a crisis vary. Certainly problems are commonplace in business. What differentiates routine dilemmas from all crises is the potential crisis has for severe damage to an organization, its employees, products, services, financial condition, and reputation.

Areas to consider include industrial accidents, environmental problems, government regulatory problems, workplace violence, union relations or strikes, natural disasters, product recalls, investor relations, hostile takeovers, rumors, acts of terrorism and embezzlement.

Make a contact sheet. The plan should list all phone numbers for team members — business, home, mobile, pager, FAX, and vacation home. It should also designate who will contact team members in the event of a crisis, and backups for team members in case one or more of them is not immediately available.

Designate a crisis control center. Consider where the team will gather during the crisis. Are there adequate phone lines? Under crisis duress, companies find that telecommunication is one area they're unprepared to handle. You may want to set up a toll free line so consumers and others can call directly to get information rather than relying on rumor. Besides planning how you will quickly connect extra phone lines, consider whether you have enough computers and other necessary equipment. What if the building is heavily damaged — is an off-site or mobile office available?

Also plan where you want the media to assemble during the crisis. You need to keep them away from sensitive areas while at the same time giving them controlled access to spokespersons and pictures of the scene.

Secondary contact sheet. List phone numbers for consultants and other experts you can summon if needed. These might include trauma counselors, security personnel, a bomb expert, technical experts, a photographer, or a telecommunications expert.

In addition, list other stakeholders who might need to be informed of the crisis such as government officials, insurance agents, distributors, vendors, managers at the "home office," and board members.

Document the crisis. Because of the possibility of future litigation and the many questions that interested parties will ask, an organization should document all events surrounding a crisis. Include pre-printed forms in the CMP to enable managers to list when and where the incident occurred, who was called when, what time the evacuation order was given, how many people were on site at the time of the incident, etc.

Also the CMP should list a clipping service to contact which will provide all newspaper articles as well as radio and TV stories about the crisis. In addition, you may want to contact a photographer to document the crisis and your response on film or video.

List action steps. Include actions that must be taken in each crisis. Should fire, police or emergency preparedness officials be called? Have victims' families been contacted? Is someone visiting their homes? Do you need to cancel advertising? Should you temporarily stop trading of the stock? Should you contact suppliers or customers? Who is communicating to employees?

Crisis Management Simulation. Having

a plan is only one part of the equation for success in crisis management. Organizations should also practice resolving crises using their CMP. By simulating various scenarios, each team member can then role play how he or she would react. A facilitator can role play outside actions that would demand reactions from the team such as a call from a reporter, a newspaper article written about the crisis, a call from the company's largest stockholder, a request for a meeting with the union officer, complaints from the town's mayor.

During the role play, an observer should record the team's reactions, statements and suggestions. After the crisis simulation, the team can then evaluate what parts of the plan didn't work and make appropriate changes to the CMP.

Communicating in Crisis

The effectiveness of an organization's communication strategy during a crisis has a direct impact on how well it and its reputation survive. Consider all your critical audiences as you do your planning: Employees and their families, customers, neighbors, stockholders, investors, suppliers, competitors, regulators, government officials, board of directors and any other groups who need to be informed about your activities.

The most important group to consider in your communication plan is the news media, a conduit to many of your other audiences. Reporters can be your best friends in a crisis, helping to disseminate important information, accurately conveying your messages to the public. Or the media can be your worst enemies, attacking your credibility, questioning your sincerity, and second guessing you. Much depends on whether they believe you are being open and honest with them, and whether you have planned carefully how you will deal with reporters.

Choose a spokesperson. One person — a good communicator who has been media trained — should handle the bulk of media interviews during a crisis. This helps ensure the message will be consistent. The CEO should also be visible, perhaps appearing at a news conference or issuing a statement. The CEO should also consider going to the scene of the crisis, if appropriate. As we mentioned earlier, one of the criticisms that continues to haunt Exxon after the oil spill is that CEO Lawrence Rawl didn't immediately travel to Alaska to confront the situation first hand.

React quickly. The sooner you speak to the media in a crisis, the less time there is for speculation and inaccuracies to be reported. This was NASA's first communication mistake in the *Challenger* explosion. Even if you have little information, you must be open and available to reporters to tell them that.

Show empathy and concern. This is a key ingredient of crisis communication. You can express empathy ("Our hearts go out to victims' friends and family.") without accepting blame. You can also show concern ("We're concerned about the situation. We thought we had done everything to prevent it, and we'll be reassessing that.") This was another criticism of Exxon — company officials didn't seem to care about the pollution of Prince William Sound. Don't fake concern, though. Honest emotion (except for uncontrolled anger) is appropriate.

Offer immediate assistance to any victims and their families. Depending on the specific crisis, this could include paying for medical care, arranging temporary housing, or recalling a defective product.

Determine key messages. To formulate your key communication messages, first consider who your main audience is and what your goal is in the communication. Do you want to calm people, persuade them, inform them or alert them to possible danger?

Anticipate questions. What the media doesn't understand, it expresses with outrage. It's up to you to explain, in a way reporters can understand, the details of your crisis. Be prepared to answer the five W's: Who was involved? What happened? When did it happen? Where did it happen? Why did it happen? Also be prepared to address what precautions you took to prevent the crisis, what you are doing right now to remedy the situation, and how you will make sure it doesn't happen again.

Don't speculate. When facts are scarce or slow in coming, and reporters are pressing you for information, it's tempting to guess at what did happen or will happen. Don't! This will only fuel rumors and premature conclusions.

Don't lie to or mislead reporters. The media will likely discover your untruthfulness. This will destroy your credibility with reporters and the public.

SoundBites

Hold regular briefings. Continually update reporters. If there is nothing new, tell them that directly. The media need constant information as they write or report new stories. If you don't keep them briefed, they will go elsewhere for information and you lose control of the story.

Admit mistakes. Take responsibility and apologize when it's obvious you are at fault. Tell how you will fix the problem so that it doesn't happen again. This tactic can go a long way toward calming a crisis. Stonewalling rarely gets you anywhere.

Don't accuse or blame. To accuse or blame is to court libel or slander. You will appear defensive and uncaring. Accept responsibility for your conduct and avoid talking about others' actions. People admired President Harry Truman for his "the buck stops here" attitude.

Determine what you can't say. Your crisis management plan should remind managers and spokespersons that certain information **must** be kept confidential. This may include private information about employees and proprietary information about the company such as net worth or ingredients of products.

Have background information available. Keep a supply of press kits ready to give to reporters if a crisis occurs. Include company fact sheets, still pictures, product information, and other pertinent information.

Control the news conference. At some point, you will probably have to use news conferences as a way to speak to a large number of reporters at one time. Make sure you have proper security and that reporters have press credentials.

Maintain a sense of calm and control during the news conference. You can help your spokesperson(s) prepare with a rehearsal. Give several people the role of reporter and let the spokesperson practice fielding their questions.

Managing a Cybercrisis

As much as the Internet creates excitement about new ways to communicate, there's a dark side to this emerging medium. In today's electronic world it is possible for almost anyone to single-handedly create controversy or harm your company's image by using the Internet. Computer- and Internet-savvy individuals can quickly disseminate their negative message as loudly and effectively as a huge corporation.

A case in point is McDonald's. When the company sued two people who published a fact sheet on the Internet entitled "What's Wrong With McDonald's?" a group of activists retaliated by creating an anti-McDonald's Web site called McSpotlight to provide the press and public with

SoundBites

information on the ongoing libel trial. They were very successful. In a 12-week period the site had more than 41,000 visitors, many of whom were journalists seeking information about the trial.

Companies can't afford to ignore or underestimate attacks and potential crises on the Internet. In order to react quickly, someone in your organization should regularly surf the Web and monitor newsgroups that talk about your company and industry.

Treat an attack like a true media crisis by immediately responding. Try to reach the source of the attacks so you can tell your side of the story and clear up misleading or inaccurate information. Also respond with your own Web page and to the online media, as well as traditional media outlets.

I began this chapter by citing crises as endemic, the everyday condition of being human. I close it by borrowing from a Lincolnesque lawyer no longer able to speak for himself. With legal nicety before a gathering of his peers, he recounted a range of human crises he had dealt with in his distinguished career: clients overtaken by serious illness, foreclosures, divorce, death; organizations forced into bankruptcy. And he ended his talk by arguing that above all else, a sense of humor was required, whatever the stress, however great the crisis. "I have," he said in closing soundbite, "done much work with wills and like many of you here, I have discovered that where there's a will there's a way."

Chapter 9

Glory in the Soundbite

"Everybody should have a dream."
Jesse Owens

In these pages, you and I have celebrated soundbites as the currency of modern media communication. In some detail we have examined soundbites that transmit the basic human truths by which we live and by which the daily fare of business and commerce is conveyed. In this age of speed-up, down-sizing, redesigning and re-engineering, soundbites set the beat for our daily lives and govern public communication at its best. Those soundbites that work — we have shown — are distinguished by their five C's: they are clear, concise, conversational, catchy, and colorful.

With these five C's firmly in mind, with some practice in using them to make soundbites that dance with meaning and impact in our speaking to the media, it is time to turn to a sixth "C," the most important of them all, and the one whose mastery will mean the most in our lives. That "C" stands for Creativity. It was not by accident or chance that this book began with the name of Lincoln, soon to be followed by the gifted Greek poet Sappho and by Socrates and Plato and so on through a host of greats, all of whom were distinguished by and shared one talent: they were

SoundBites

Creative — Creative with a capital "C."

How, you ask, does one become Creative? The answer is simple and complex, though it will come as a surprise to many. You were born Creative, unique in time and space. The moment you begin testifying to your uniqueness in your response to the world, you will find yourself Creative. That is the simple part. The complex part demands further explanation, for you and I know that by and large we are not surrounded by Creative people although each person may have been born to be Creative. And here I will turn to a mythical child to explain the mystery of being Creative.

We will name her "Kay," a short name that identifies her as she sees herself. Born into an average family living in an average house in an average American community, she was fed, loved, cared for and reared to be a commonplace American who would fit in, belong to class, school, group, be interchangeable with any other average American of her race, age, gender and community. But a strange thing occurred in Kay's life. Without her planning it, her household was one of hardworking, caring parents and in that household she became aware that her parents were unusual people. Her father — call him "Bill," sometimes "Bill-due," the price he paid for food, clothing and keeping the roof on the modest family house — was a dreamer who quickly let Kay know he expected her to perform in unusual ways. He said, "Kay, I want you to live up to your genes, I

Chapter Nine

want you to be a reader, a thinker, a doer."

Kay listened to what he said but in her mind she asked, "Why — and how?"

Kay's mother Sue was a fit mate for Bill. She showed how she felt about him and Kay by the way she cared for them — cooking, cleaning, cajoling, loving, and in quiet moments working on her art that she called "needlepoint." In fact, she hung on the wall of the living room a needlepoint by which she said Kay might live her life. The needlepoint contained words and fruits and vegetables, the words "Live Within Your Harvest" in red encircling the fruits and vegetables: apples, cherries, grapes, peaches, pears, plums, blueberries, melons, carrots, beets, zucchini, lettuce, tomatoes — a plethora of color and greenery.

Like most children, Kay was curious and impatient, and it took years for the message from her mother's needlepoint to sink in, to work its intended effect. This despite Bill and Sue's telling her time and again when she climbed down from the school bus defeated and tired, "Kay dear, read, think, and do, so that you can live within your harvest."

Time passed — as it will — and Kay found herself in college where her best teachers, whatever their subject, told her again, "Read, think, and do so that you can live within your harvest." Kay listened and found their messages brought to her mind a needlepoint in a distant Pennsylvania household and as she reflected on that scene, the message etched itself into her mind, became

265

SoundBites

a part of her being. Then came the day another teacher spoke to her, saying, "Kay, read, think, write and speak so that you can live within your harvest, become one with those you respect and love."

Kay waited for him to add the biblical trapping, "As ye sow so shall ye reap," but he was one who knew when to let well enough alone, to permit the creative spark to build to flame that would light a darkened world. Kay listened, smiled, and sat down at her computer to shape an enduring soundbite.

About the Author

Kathy Kerchner is a seven-time Emmy award winner and communications expert. During 14 years as a television news reporter and anchor, she interviewed thousands of people including a president — Gerald Ford; politicians — former Vice President Dan Quayle, former Senator Barry Goldwater, Senator John McCain, former Governor, presidential candidate, and now Secretary of the Interior Bruce Babbitt; and celebrities — Dick Clark, Ann Landers, Barbara Bush, Buster Crabbe, and Joe Garagiola.

While working at network affiliates in Indiana, California and Arizona, Kerchner covered stories that took her outside the United States to Mexico, Japan, Guam, Bolivia, and twice to the Amazon Region of Brazil.

Since 1989, she has worked as a speaker, trainer and consultant through her company Kathy Kerchner InterSpeak, Inc. in Scottsdale, Arizona. She does coaching, workshops and speeches on successful media interviewing, communicating in a crisis, and making presentations that connect with and persuade any size audience. She also gives keynote speeches on topics related to business and personal change.

Kerchner's clients have included Fortune 500 companies, businesses, associations and government agencies: Motorola, Dial Corp., Phelps Dodge, Cyprus Amax, Intel, American Medical Association, National Association of Homes and Services for the Aging, American Institute of CPA's, National Association of Purchasing Management, Maricopa Association of Governments, Arizona Department of Economic Security, Sandia National Laboratories, and Supreme Court of Virginia. She has worked with clients internationally in Canada, Spain, Hong Kong and Switzerland.

Kathy Kerchner holds a Bachelor of Arts degree in English from Denison University and a Master of Arts degree in Communications from The University of Michigan. In addition to her book, *SoundBites: a Business Guide for Working with the Media*, she is the author of an audio cassette program, *Master the Media*.

Index

Absolutes, as a soundbite, 23-24
Actualities, 140
Agenda, interview, 153-159, 163-164
Ainge, Danny, 97
Ambush interview, 146-147
Analogies, as a soundbite, 22
Anchor, television, 55-56
Anchor interview, 196, 221-222
Aramony, William, 251
Armstrong, Neil, 23
Ashland Oil, 247-249
Assignment editor, television, 54-55
Attitude, vocal communication, 207
Audi, 71
Audience, interview,158

Bailey, F. Lee, 22
Bentsen, Lloyd, 15-16
Body language, 203
Book of Job, 230
Bridges, 163-166
    example, 165
British Petroleum oil spill, 182
Broadcast editor, wire service, 65-66
Brown, Ron, death of, 96
Bureau chief
        newspaper, 59-60
        wire service, 65
Burke, James, 244
Bush, George, 23, 27, 34, 35

Index

Challenger space shuttle, 91, 95, 236-237
Chase's Annual Events, 104
Checkers Speech, 232
Cheney, Dick, 36-37
Chrysler, 104
Churchill, Winston, 38
City Editor, newspaper, 58-59
Clark, Marcia, 29
Cliches, as a soundbite, 22-23
Clinton, Bill, 19, 24, 34
Clothing, 199-200
Cochran, Johnnie, 16
Coleridge, Samuel Taylor, 189
Columnist, newspaper, 60-61
Communication
     crisis, 257-260
     nonverbal, 189-211
     Three Vs, 191-192
       verbal, 191-192
       visual, 192-204
       vocal, 204-210
Community section editor, newspaper, 59-60
Conciseness, interview, 18, 175-178
Contemporary references, as a soundbite, 21-22
Coolness, in an interview, 178-180
Coors Beer, 71
Corrections, 183-184
Crisis communication,257-260
Crisis control center, 254-255
Crisis management, 230-262
     Ashland Oil, 247-249
     Challenger space shuttle,236-237
     cyberspace, 261-262

Exxon Valdez, 233-235
Jack in the Box, 237-240
Luby's Cafeteria, 249-250
McDonalds, 261
NASA, 236-237
news conference, 261
Pepsi-Cola, 245-246
response team, 253
risk assessment, 253-254
simulation, 256-257
spokesperson, 257-258
TWA Flight 800, 240-242
Tylenol, 242-245
United Way, 250-252
Crisis management plan, 253-255
Cyberspace
crisis management, 261-262
interview in, 226-227
media relations in, 128-130

Daybook, wire service, 66
Deadline, 46, 107-109
Decker, Bert, 191
DeConcini, Dennis, 27,36

Editor, newspaper, 59
Editorial Board, meeting, 223-224
Editorial page, newspaper, 61
Emotions, as a soundbite, 20-21
Erben, Pete, 249-250
Erickson, Jeffrey, 240-242

Index

Errors, correcting, 74-78, 183-184
Evaluation, interview, 227-229
Examples
    bridges, 165
    fact sheet, 124-126
    interview preparation checklist, 159-162
    media advisory, 121-123
    media kit contents, 127
    media list, 107
    news release, 114-120
    news release, feature, 116-120
    Post-Interview Evaluation, 228-229
    press kit contents, 127
    Public Service Announcement, 136-138
Examples, as a soundbite, 21
Exxon Valdez oil spill, 182, 233-235
Eye contact, 196-197, 203

Face, 195-196
Fact sheet, 124-126
Fields, W.C., 102
Five C's of Success, 17-20
Flagging, 183
Furman, Mark, 178

Gelbert, Debra, 79
Gestures, 197-198
Gingrich, Newt, 21
Goldwater, Barry, 26
Grooming, 200-201

Haig, Alexander, 35
Hall, John, 248
Hart, Bill, 176
Head, 197
Helms, Jesse, 36
Henson, Jim, 102
Hitler, Adolph, 38
Home page, news release, 130
Hooks, news, 91-98
Hopkins, Gerard Manley, 88
Humor, as a soundbite, 24-25

I don't know, 185
Inflection, 205-206
Information, off the record, 73-74
Interview
       advanced questions, 153
       agenda, 152-159, 163-166
       ambush, 146-147
       audience, 158
       attacks in, 186-187, 260
       buying time, 144-147
       conciseness in, 175-178
       control of, 163-188
       coolness in,178-180
       corporate information, 152
       empathy in,172-173
       evaluation of, 227-229
       Four Steps of Preparation, 144
       flagging, 183
       holding ground in, 169-172
       hostile questions, 151

Index

invert the triangle, 173-175
key message in, 155-158
know the territory, 147-150
limitations, 158-159
media message in, 163-166
microphone in, 210-211
negative language in, 166-169
nightmare, 152
off the record, 73-74
positive, 166-169
preparation for, 142-162
preparation checklist, 159-162
questions, 150-153
refusing an, 70-72
reporter's name, 187-188
silence in, 185-186, 209
speculation in, 182-183
strength in, 163-188
uninformed questions, 151-152
Interviews, types of
    cyberspace, 226-227
    editorial board, 223-224
    live on-set television, 219
    live television, 217-219
    national television news magazine, 71-72
    news conference, 213-216
    newspaper, 222-223
    magazine, 222-223
    print, 222-224
    radio, 224-226
    radio talk show, 224-225
    taped television news, 216-217
    telephone, 207-210

SoundBites

television, 216-222
television anchor, 196, 221-222
television talk show, 220-221
Invert the triangle, 173-175

Jack in the Box, 237-240
Jargon, in interview, 180
Jefferson, Thomas, 18
Johnson & Johnson, 242-245
Jordon, Michael, 21
Journalism, confrontational, 146
Joyce, James, 88

KDKA Radio, 61
Kennedy, John F., 16
King, Martin Luther, 39
King, Rodney, 139
Kuralt, Charles, 102

Limitations, interview, 158-159
Lincoln, Abraham, 9, 39
Live on-set interview, 219
Live radio interview, 225-226
Live television interview, 217-219
Location, visual communication, 194-195
Luby's Cafeteria, 249-250

Magazine, interview, 222-223
Make-up, 201-202

Index

Managing editor, newspaper, 58
Manners, microphone, 210-211
Mays, Bob, 23
McDonalds, 261
McNamara, Robert, 36
Mecham, Evan, 35
Media, reporters, 46-66
Media Advisory, 121-123
Media interview, 212-229
Media kit, 126-127
Media list, 105-107
      example, 107
Media needs
      print news, 140-141
      radio news, 140
      television news, 138-140
Media relations, cyberspace, 128-130
Media relationships, 38-45, 79-85
Message, key, 155-158
Metro editor, newspaper, 58-59
Microphone
      manners, 210-211
      news conference, 211
      on camera, 210
      on radio, 210
      speech, 211
Mistakes
      corrections to, 74-78
      admitting, 182, 260
Mondale, Walter, 21
Murphy's Law, 230

SoundBites

NASA, 236-237
Negligible Nibbles, 26-33
News
    audience of, 94
    conflict in, 95-96
    credibility, 98
    definition of, 89-90
    fame, 96-97
    hooks, 91-98
    human interest, 94-95
    magnitude of, 92-93
    print, needs, 140-141
    progress, 96
    proximity of, 94
    radio, needs, 140
    significance of, 91-92
    television, needs, 138-140
    timeliness of, 93
    unusualness, 97
News categories, 98-104
    helpful information, 103
    holidays, 104
    hot issues, 101
    interesting items, 102
    kids/animals, 102
    local, 99-100
    sidebars, 100-101
    special events, 102-103
    spot news, 104
    success/failure/turnaround, 103-104
    trends, 101-102
News conference, 213-216
    crisis, 261

Index

location, 214
scheduling, 214
spokesperson, 215
visual aids, 215
written statement, 215
News director
radio, 63
television, 53
News editor, wire service, 65
News release, 109-120
advertising in, 109
cyberspace, 128-130
e-mail, 128-130
example of, 114-120
fax, 131
feature, example of, 116-120
follow-up, 130-131
format, 112-114
home page, 130
personal meeting, 131-132
Public Service Announcement, 134-138
video, 132-133
Newspaper
bureau chief, 59-60
city editor, 58-59
columnist, 60-61
community section editor, 59-60
editor, 59
editorial page, 61
interview, 222-223
managing editor, 59
publisher, 58
reporter, 60

SoundBites

Newsroom, 33-42
      newspaper, 57-61
      radio, 61-64
      television, 53-57
      wire service, 64-66
NewsSpeak Quiz, 85-87
Nightmare, interview, 152
Nixon, Richard, 166, 182, 232-233
Nixon/Kennedy presidential debates, 189-190
No comment, 66-69
Nonverbal communication , 189-211

Off the record, 73-74
Oklahoma City bombing, 92, 95, 100
Olivier, Laurence, 143-144
One-Liners, as a soundbite, 23
Owens, Jesse, 263

Pace, 206
Pause, in interview, 181
Pepsi-Cola, 245-246
Perot, Ross, 22, 25, 34
Personal experiences, as a soundbite, 20-21
Photographer, television, 57
Photographs, 127-128
Plato, 14
Pope John Paul, 101
Posture, 198-199
Press kit, 126-127
Print

Index

interview, 222-224
news needs, 140-141
Producer
radio, 64
television, 54
Proportional numbers, as a soundbite, 24
Public Service Announcement, 134-138
example, 136-138
Publisher, newspaper, 58

Quayle, Dan, 199-200
Questions, 150-153
hostile, 151
uninformed, 151-152
Quiz, NewsSpeak, 85-87
Quoting opposition, as a soundbite, 24

Radio
interview, 224-226
news director, 63
news needs, 140
newsroom, 61-64
producer, 64
reporter, 63
talk show host, 63-64
Radio talk show, 224-225
Rawl, Lawrence, 235
Reagan, Ronald, 22, 25
Reporters
and interviews, 142-144
and negativity, 48

as generalists, 47-47
deadlines, 107-109
fairness, 49-50
media, 46-66
newspaper, 60
radio, 63
television, 56-57
Response team, crisis, 253
Ripken, Cal, 100
Risk assessment, in a crisis, 253-254
Roosevelt, Franklin Delano, 23, 38, 231

San Francisco earthquake, 92-93, 95
Sappho, 13
Sargent, Clair, 19-20
Satellite Media Tour, 133-134
Schwartzkopf, Norman, 25
Silence, in an interview, 185-186, 209
Simpson, O.J., trial, 16, 22, 29, 100, 178
Simulation, crisis management, 256-257
Socrates, 13-14
Soundbite
average length, 10
catchy, 19
clear, 17-18
colorful, 19-20
concise, 18
controversy, 33-37
conversational, 18-19
definition, 14
negligible nibbles, 26-37
printed form, 15

Index

radio, 140
stupidity, 33-37
successful, 17, 26-33
television, 139-140
what gets soundbited, 20-25
Speaker phone, interview, 209
Speculation, 182-183
Spokesperson
    and accessibility, 79-80
    and cooperation, 79
    and directness, 80
    and fairness, 80-81
    as a resource, 81
    as a strategist, 83-84
    as a team player, 84-85
    as an advocate, 83
    as an authority, 82
    as an educator, 82
    crisis, 257-258
    news conference, 215
Stein, Gertrude, 88
Stockdale, General, 34
Super Bowl, 101

Talking head, 15
Talk show host, radio, 63-64
Taped interview, 216-217, 225-226
Telephone interview, 207-209
Television
    anchor, 55-56
    anchor interview, 196, 221-222
    assignment editor, 54-55

SoundBites

    interview, 216-222
    live interview, 217-219
    live on-set interview, 219
    news director, 53
    news needs, 138-140
    photographer, 57
    producer, 54
    reporter, 56-57
    talk show interview, 220-221
    taped news interview, 216-217
Television newsroom, 53-57
Television talk show, interview, 220-221
TWA Flight 800, 240-242
Tylenol poisoning, 242-245

United Way, 250-252
USA Today, 15

Verbal communication, 191-192
Video news release, 132-133
Visual aids, 203-204
Visual communication, 194-204
    authority, 194
    clothing, 199-200
    concern, 194
    eye contact, 196-197
    face, 195-196
    gestures, 197-198
    grooming, 200-201
    head, 197

Index

location, 194-195
make-up, 201-202
openness, 194
posture, 198-199
print, 203
television, 192-202
visual aids, 203-204
Vocal communication, 204-210
attitude, 206
inflection, 205-206
pace, 206
volume, 206

Watergate, 48, 233
Weatherup, Craig, 246
White, E.B., 102
Wilder, Governor, 98
Wire service
broadcast editor, 65-66
bureau chief, 65
daybook, 66
news editor, 65
newsroom, 64-66

Ordering Information

To order additional copies of

SoundBites:
A Business Guide for
Working with the
Media,

or to inquire about

speeches, seminars, and workshops

contact:

Kathy Kerchner InterSpeak, Inc.
11025 N. Miller Road
Scottsdale, AZ 85260

Phone: (602) 998-3214
FAX: (602) 998-0198

Other Books Available from Savage Press

Hometown Wisconsin by Marshall J. Cook

Treasures from the Beginning of the World by Jeff Lewis

Stop in the Name of the Law by Alex O'Kash

A Hint of Frost — Essays from the Earth by Rusty King

Widow of the Waves by Bev Jamison

Superior Catholics by Cheney & Meronek

Gleanings from the Hillsides by E.M. Johnson

Keeper of the Town by Don Cameron

Thicker Than Water by Hazel Sangster

Moments Beautiful Moments Bright
by Brett Bartholomaus

The Courtship of Sarah McClean by S & S Castleberry

Some Things You Never Forget by Clem Miller

The Year of the Buffalo,
a novel of love and minor league baseball
by Marshall J. Cook

Appalachian Mettle by Paul Bennett

Beyond the Mine — A Steelworker's Story
by Pete Benzoni

To order copies of
any
Savage Press book

or receive the complete
Savage Press catalog,

contact us at:

Tel: 1-800-732-3867
Voice and Fax: (715) 394-9513
e-mail: savpress@spacestar.com
Web Page
www.cp.duluth.mn.us/~awest/savpress

Visa or MasterCard accepted.

Savage
PRESS

Box 115, Superior, WI 54880 (715) 394-9513

We are always looking for good manuscripts—
poetry, fiction, memoirs, family history, true crime
and other genres. Send a synopsis and the first three
chapters.